American Language Hub

LEVEL 5A
Student's Book

JEREMY DAY
GRAHAM SKERRITT
KIERAN DONAGHY

macmillan education

Contents

Welcome

GRAMMAR

Verb tenses and structures

A **Choose the correct option to complete the conversation.**

A: Hello. Could you tell me [1]*where is the conversation class* / *where the conversation class is*?

B: Yes, just follow me! [2]*I'm going* / *I'll go* there now. I actually study here myself.

A: Cool. [3]*Did you* / *Have you* been studying English for long?

B: Let me think. Actually [4]*I'll have been* / *I'll be* at this school for two years at the end of this month. Don't worry. You [5]*don't have to* / *must not* bring anything. Just yourself. And there is only one rule: you [6]*don't need to* / *must not* speak in your own language in class.

A: Great, that's really important. In my last school we [7]*used to* / *get used to* do a lot of grammar. But I wasn't [8]*taught* / *didn't teach* any speaking or pronunciation. So I really need to [9]*used to* / *get used to* speaking more.

B: Yes, me too. I [10]*was learning* / *am learning* on my own for a little while, but stopped because I didn't feel like I'd made much progress.

Articles, determiners and quantifiers

B **Find and correct the mistakes in the sentences.**

1 It's ~~the~~ good to watch videos in English to practice your listening.
2 A lot problems when learning a language come from lack of confidence not lack of ability.
3 It's best to get personal recommendations when finding the English courses.
4 When you first learn a language you should spend a great deal time on grammar.
5 A childhood is a good time to start learning a language.
6 There's never time enough when you're working and learning at the same time.
7 Most the people feel demotivated at some point when learning a new language.
8 Every languages has it own unique pronunciation and grammar and you can't easily compare them.
9 Languages are neither fixed and completely stable but are constantly changing.

C **SPEAK** **Work in pairs and discuss the questions.**

1 Do you agree with the speakers in Exercise A? Why/Why not?
2 Do you agree with the statements in Exercise B? Why/Why not?

VOCABULARY

Collocations

A **Choose the correct words to complete the collocations.**

1 It's *highly* / *deeply* / *absolutely* likely that even jobs in education will be automated in the future.
2 Concerning future problems, I'm *bitterly* / *deeply* / *ridiculously* concerned about extreme weather conditions.
3 There is the possibility *for* / *of* / *about* colonizing another planet to relieve human overpopulation.
4 Young people should have *knowledge* / *ideas* / *opinions* of news sources and searching online to deal with the problem of fake news.
5 Understanding your *focus* / *target* / *regular* audience is important for being an entrepreneur.
6 Not all regeneration projects get a *positive* / *high* / *key* reaction from local communities.

Compound adjectives and nouns

B **Complete the sentences with the compound adjectives and nouns in the box.**

community spirit	last-minute	old-fashioned
six-bedroom	street parties	up-to-date

1 Visit our website for the most ________ travel times and ________ deals.
2 Mark and Susan have just bought a huge ________ house in the country. It's a little ________, but they're planning on renovating it.
3 There is great ________ in my town. The local council usually organize ________ for national holidays.

C **SPEAK** **Work in pairs. Do you agree with the statements in Exercise A?**

PRONUNCIATION

0.1 **A** **Circle the arrows to predict which intonation will be used. Then listen and check.**

1 Is this meeting finishing soon? [↗] / [↘]
2 How often do you come to these classes? [↗] / [↘]
3 Unless there is a good reason [↗] / [↘], you shouldn't work late. [↗] / [↘]
4 Take some chocolate bars [↗] / [↘], in case you need a quick snack. [↗] / [↘]

0.2 **B** **Listen to the sentences. Draw (‿) between any words that link together.**

1 He's improved a lot despite having a few problems.
2 We went out at night a lot to see the city.
3 Plenty of people find it difficult at first.
4 Hundreds of people came out to see her talk.

C **Practice saying the sentences in Exercise B.**

1 TRENDS

> The majority have no other reason for their opinions than that they are the fashion.
>
> Samuel Johnson

A flamingo among geese, egrets, swans and herons.

OBJECTIVES

- talk about style and fashion
- give fashion advice
- compare different trends
- make a podcast or vlog
- pitch your own business idea
- write a blog post

Work with a partner. Discuss the questions.

1 Look at the picture. How does it relate to trends?

2 Read the quote. What do you think it means? Do you agree?

3 How important are trends in the following areas to you?

- fashion
- music
- design
- lifestyle

1.1 Dress for success

- Talk about style and fashion
- Give fashion advice

V– clothes and fashion; metaphors G– nominal clauses P– linking /r/ S– listening for recommendations

VOCABULARY
Clothes and fashion

A Work in pairs. Take the quiz.

B Go to the **Vocabulary Hub** on **page 142**.

1 Do you carefully plan your **outfits** or just wear the first thing on hand?
2 Have you ever had to attend an event with **a dress code**?
3 If you had to go to a **costume** party, what costume would you wear?
4 Are people more productive when they wear a **uniform** or **casual** clothing?
5 Would you describe yourself as a **trendsetter** or a **trend follower**?
6 Is it better to **fit in with** or **stand out** from **the crowd**?
7 Do you ever wear **baggy** or **scruffy** clothes to relax at home?

READING

A **PREDICT** Work in pairs. Read the title of the article. Look at pictures 1–3. How might what the people are wearing affect their behavior?

B **SCAN** Read *Style speaks* and check your predictions from Exercise A.

STYLE *speaks*

We've all heard the old adages … *Dress for the job you want, not the job you have. Look good, feel good.* These clichés are somewhat worn out. How can the way we dress affect our lives? But it seems there may be some truth in them after all. People do form first impressions based on what we're wearing. Not only that but maybe even part of our own self-worth is tied up in the clothing choices we make.

1

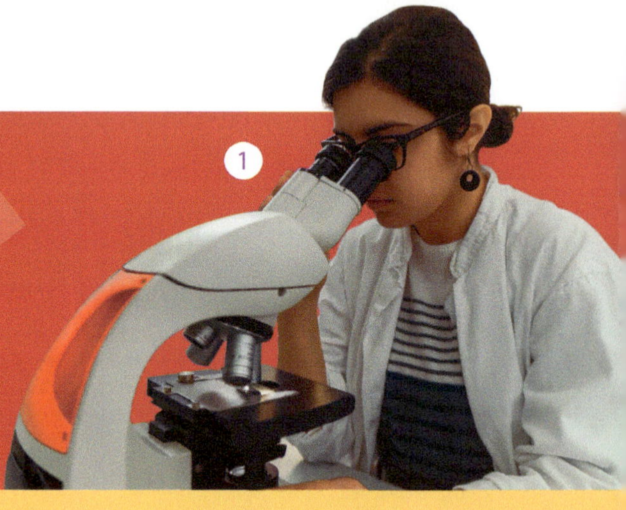

Power dressing

Not convinced? Imagine turning up for an interview at a big city firm, or company in the jeans you've been wearing for the past three days and an old baggy T-shirt. Would you be successful in getting the job? Unlikely. Would you feel self-conscious about what you're wearing? Very likely. It seems that wearing dress clothes, such as a well-made suit, could help you feel more confident. And when we're feeling confident we negotiate better, we respond better to questions and we put other people at ease.

2

Breaking free

On the flip side, wearing fitted or tailored clothing is not what most of us would choose to wear when we are trying to be creative. Can you imagine writing the next great novel, or coming up with a great innovation while sitting and typing away in a $2,000 designer suit? This is why many leading tech companies have an ultra-relaxed dress code and encourage casual clothing. Mark Zuckerberg isn't topping any best-dressed lists but his billions of dollars make up for it. Furthermore, many workplaces have 'Casual Fridays' to encourage employees to let their hair down a little and get creativity flowing.

Uniform thinking

Wearing a uniform can make us feel part of something – provide us with a sense of belonging, but also one of duty. Many people argue that wearing school uniforms encourages us to work harder. While this is not necessarily true, there is no doubt that when, for example, a firefighter puts on a helmet or a doctor puts on a white coat, it comes with a responsibility. So fundamentally, to dress the role is to start to live it.

Glossary

adage (n) a well-known phrase that says something about life and human experience
clique (n) a small group of people who seem unfriendly to other people
unconsciously (adv) without realizing or being aware of one's actions

C READ FOR DETAIL Read the article again. Complete each statement with one to three words from the article.

1 People should wear ________________ when they're feeling down.
2 ________________ could help people come up with new ideas.
3 People sometimes wear ________________ clothing to fit in.
4 ________________ may encourage people to make healthier choices.
5 People should wear ________________ to feel more persuasive.
6 ________________ may make people more careful at work.

D SPEAK Discuss in small groups.

1 What surprised you most about the blog post?
2 Do you think your own choice of clothes affects how you think and behave?

Gym ready

It's not just work that clothing affects, but lifestyle as well. Professional and semi-professional athletes tend to stick rigidly to an 'athleisure' style. Their reasoning? They don't enjoy wearing formal clothes. And they want to be able to work out whenever they feel like it. And for many, having the clothes on reminds them to make healthier choices … to choose the fruit salad over the fruit pie.

Pack mentality

Have we really evolved that much away from our primal, tribal instincts? Visit any city center at lunchtime on a Saturday and your answer will be probably not. The packs of roving teenagers are dressed in a pseudo uniform of name-brand clothing, like Ray-Bans and Hollister T-shirts. We unconsciously imitate the clothing of people we look up to. A shared sense of style builds rapport and helps you to instantly feel part of a clique. Maybe it's self-preservation, or maybe it's a hope that you will be infused with the qualities you admire.

Lift your mood

That our mood impacts what we choose to wear will not come as a surprise. How many of us think about it the other way around? What we wear could affect how we are feeling for the better or worse. One of the best cures for when you're feeling down is to wear that cozy, bright yellow sweater. More people than you might think are great believers in wearing bright colors to boost positivity. It seems simple, but why not give it a shot next time you're having a bad day?

GRAMMAR

Nominal clauses

A Read the sentences. Is the underlined part of each sentence the subject or the object?

1 They don't enjoy <u>wearing formal clothes</u>.
2 <u>Wearing a uniform</u> can make us feel part of something.

B Work in pairs. Underline the nominal clauses in sentences from the article. Use the information in the box to help you. The first two have been done for you.

Nominal clauses

Nominal clauses are clauses that work like nouns. They are very common as objects, but they are also possible as the subject, after a preposition or the verb *be*, and in the following ways.

a nominal *-ing* clause ___
b nominal *that* clause ___
c nominal question-clause ___
d nominal infinitive ___
e We frequently use a phrase like *the fact/idea that* or *the experience/problem of* to introduce a nominal clause and make it easier to understand. ___
f *That* clauses and infinitive can sound unnatural as the subject. We can use *it* as an empty subject instead. ___

1 Luke is upset <u>that he didn't pass</u>.
2 Lisa doesn't enjoy <u>watching horror movies</u>.
3 It wasn't surprising that Tara came in first place.
4 The fact that the team won the tournament shows how good the manager is.
5 Where you go to college is your choice.
6 To tell a lie about something so important was wrong.

C WORK IT OUT Match sentences 1–6 in Exercise B with the rules (a–f) in the box.

D Go to the **Grammar Hub** on **page VI**.

E Complete the sentences so they are true for you. Then discuss in pairs.

1 What I like doing most of all in the evenings …
2 How a person is dressed …
3 Spending a lot of money on …

SPEAKING

DISCUSS Work in groups. To what extent do you agree with the following statements? Give reasons for your answers.

- Wearing a uniform affects what grades you get in school.
- Buying expensive clothes is the best way to succeed in life.
- Spending a lot of money on luxury goods makes people more generous.

LISTENING

A SPEAK Work in pairs. Look at the infographic from a fashion magazine. What do you think the results would be in your country?

1.1 **B LISTEN FOR RECOMMENDATIONS** Listen to a conversation between two friends. What nine tips does Carly give Dan? Use the information in the box to help you.

> **Listening for recommendations**
>
> When listening for recommendations, pay attention to phrases like *it's a good idea to*, *it's always worth*, or *don't forget to*.
>
> Also listen for phrases that signal a shift from main points to examples (e.g. *for instance*, *let's say*) and those that move from examples to new main points (e.g. *more generally*, *that's an example of*).

1.1 **C LISTEN FOR DETAIL** Listen again. Choose the correct answers (a, b or c).

1 Why is Dan worried?
- **a** He doesn't know what to wear for his new job.
- **b** He thinks people won't respect him.
- **c** He won't earn enough to buy nice clothes.

2 What's good about the suit Dan wants to buy?
- **a** the price
- **b** the fit
- **c** the quality

3 Why did Dan wear baggy sweatpants for his job interview?
- **a** He knew the interviewers couldn't see them.
- **b** He wanted to create a good impression.
- **c** He didn't have any other pants.

4 What should Dan do with his suit pants?
- **a** mend them
- **b** sell them
- **c** put them in the trash

5 According to Carly, what's good about ugly sales pages?
- **a** You can charge more money.
- **b** You appear inexperienced.
- **c** You can buy things cheaply.

6 Where does Carly say you can find good second-hand bargains?
- **a** expensive parts of town
- **b** trendy neighborhoods
- **c** areas near colleges

D SPEAK Work in small groups.

1 Which of Carly's tips do you already follow?

2 Would you try any of them in the future? Why/Why not?

FASHION TRENDS
in the US according to our readers

75% of you only buy **NAME-BRAND** sportswear

45% believe **QUALITY** is more important than **VALUE** for money

IMAGE is the first thing that **85%** of you notice about someone the first time you meet them

65% **THROW** ripped clothing away rather than **MENDING** it

40% of our readers think **FASHION** is more important than **COMFORT**

VOCABULARY
Metaphors

A SPEAK Work in pairs. Look at the sentences. What do the underlined words and phrases mean?

1 **a** I'd love to come out tonight, but I'm on a tight budget. ___

b They had some nice suits, but they were all too tight. ___

2 **a** The dress was so finely stitched that it looked seamless. ___

b It needs to be a seamless process for your customers. ___

3 **a** Instead of buying a cheap off-the-rack suit, save up for a tailor-made suit. ___, ___

b Don't use an off-the-shelf template for your company's website. We can design a tailor-made site to help you stand out from the competition. ___, ___

B Work in pairs. Decide whether the underlined words in Exercise A are literal (l) or metaphorical (m). Use the information in the box to help you.

Metaphors

A metaphor is a word or phrase that's used in a different context from its literal meaning. It's easier to understand a metaphor when you know the literal meaning. For example:

Literal: *There is a **breeze** outside. (= a light wind)*

Metaphorical: *It was a **breeze**! I got the job. (= easy and pleasant)*

C Complete the sentences with the correct form of the words in the box.

catch drain peanut run snap wind

1 I'm getting very ________________ up about it.
2 You're throwing money down the ________________.
3 It's much better in the long ________________.
4 Then you'll have two suits in your closet for ________________.
5 Choose a template that ________________ your eye.
6 All the best stuff will be ________________ up immediately.

D Work in pairs. What is the metaphorical meaning of each sentence in Exercise C?

E Complete the questions with the correct form of a word from Exercises A or C.

1 When one person leaves a job and another person takes over, how can they make the transition as ________________ as possible?
2 Are you the kind of person who plans for the long ________________? Or do you tend to make snap decisions?
3 Have you ever bought anything that was ________________ especially for you? Or do you always buy ________________ products?
4 Which current trends really ________________ you up?

F SPEAK Work in pairs. Discuss the questions in Exercise E.

PRONUNCIATION

Linking /r/

A Work in pairs. Read the sentences below aloud. Draw a (‿) between any words that you think are connected by a /r/ sound.

1 I saw a nice suit yesterday for 40% off.
2 You're only saving money if you buy something you need.
3 I just wore a jacket from an old suit.
4 They had no idea I was wearing sweatpants.
5 Are auction sites the best place to pick up cheap clothes?
6 Avoid stores in a trendy area or one with a lot of students.
7 Many sales clerks are authorized to offer discounts.

1.2 **B** Listen to check. Then practice saying the sentences.

SPEAKING HUB

A PREPARE Choose one of the following roles. Spend a few minutes thinking about your character (e.g. your age, background, ambitions, the problems you face, etc).

- **Role 1: The fashion victim.** You always want the latest designer fashions, but you're worried you would spend far too much.
- **Role 2: The reluctant shopper.** You hate shopping and don't care what you wear, but all your clothes are old and scruffy.
- **Role 3: The trendsetter.** You like to take risks and experiment with your clothes. Just one problem: you've run out of ideas!

B DISCUSS Work in groups of two or three. Role-play a conversation between your characters. Ask your partners for more information about their situation. Offer each other (good or bad) fashion advice.

I know it feels good to snap up a bargain, but in the long run, it's just money down the drain, don't you think?

C REFLECT Report back to the class on the best and worst advice for each character.

- Talk about style and fashion
- Give fashion advice

1.2 Trendsetting

- Compare different trends
- Make a podcast or vlog

G – comparatives and superlatives
P – emphatic stress
V – experimenting with prefixes and suffixes
S – using contrasts to work out meaning

READING

A SPEAK Work in pairs. Think of as many trends from the past five years as you can in one minute. Use the topics below to help you.

- technology
- music
- fashion
- culture

B READ FOR MAIN IDEA Read *The life cycle of a trend* quickly. Match the paragraphs (1–7) with the topics (a–d). Some paragraphs cover more than one topic.

a musical styles ___
b music formats ___, ___, ___
c games ___
d human needs ___, ___, ___

Vinyl LP Sales and Market Share

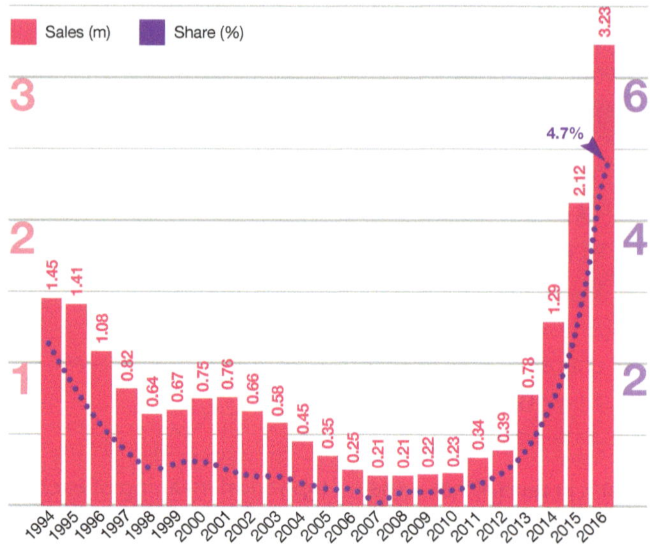

Source: British Phonographic Industry

1 Technology trends are very simple at first sight: older technologies become outdated and anachronistic, to be replaced by **newer**, **funkier** technologies, until they are rendered obsolete with the next cycle. In this way, the vinyl records of the 1970s gave way to cassettes in the 1980s. By the 1990s, cassettes were old hat and CDs were state-of-the-art. By the 2000s, we all loved novel gadgets like MP3 players. But by the 2010s, we had cloud-based music streaming services like Spotify. Why limit yourself to the music you own, when you can stream every song ever recorded?

2 But in 2016, the unexpected happened: sales of vinyl records in the UK outstripped digital music sales for the first time. The renewed interest in vinyl is a powerful reminder that trends don't always flow in a straight line from fringe products to mass-market blockbusters. It also reminds us to pay attention to the durability of trends over decades, not just the short-term ups and downs of **the latest** fads.

3 These trends are **clearest** in the world of popular music, which seems to be on a 20-year cycle. In the 1980s, music from the 50s and 60s was cool, while 70s music was tacky. By the 1990s, 70s music was enjoying a revival, but 80s music had become the height of uncool. After 2000, it was OK to like 80s music again but now 90s music was for losers. The 20-year cycle makes **somewhat more sense** when you remember that the average trendsetter is about 22 years old. They feel sheepish about the music they enjoyed when they were 12, but they can look back **a great deal more fondly** at the music from their early childhood.

4 There's a key difference between a trend, a flash-in-the-pan and a fad. A flash-in-the-pan pops up suddenly, grabs everyone's attention, and then disappears again **almost as suddenly**. A few years ago, the whole world went crazy for a new smartphone app called 'Pokémon Go'. At one point, people were playing it everywhere you looked. But within a few months, almost everybody had abandoned it, leaving only a handful of die-hard fans to persevere with it.

5 A fad, on the other hand, may be **a little more enduring**, but it too is doomed to disappear sooner or later because it serves no useful purpose. It may be quirky or amusing, but unless it fulfills a basic human need, like 'convenience', 'social status', 'self-expression' or 'security', it will never be **more than a gimmick**.

6 In contrast, an authentic trend always fulfills one of **our very deepest** needs – something that's shared by every human that's ever lived. Of course, nobody really needs **a slightly thinner than usual phone** or every song ever recorded, but we do need things like relaxation, creative stimulation, self-confidence and a sense of belonging to a social group, which those products and services satisfy.

7 This idea of basic human needs also goes some way toward explaining **by far the most curious** feature of the vinyl revival: almost half of buyers of vinyl records never actually listen to them according to a poll by ICM Unlimited! As long as we see vinyl as 'a music format' to fulfill our need for 'relaxation' and 'creative stimulation', this makes no sense. But don't forget, we also have a need to own beautiful physical objects to express our personality, and this is **every bit as important as** those other needs. And of course, the large-sleeved LPs **more than meet** that particular need, to **a much greater extent than** either diminutive CDs or intangible digital downloads.

Glossary

doom (v) to make someone or something certain to fail, be destroyed, be extremely unhappy, etc
durability (n) the ability to continue to exist or work for a long time.
outstrip (v) to become larger than something else
revival (n) the process of becoming active, successful, or popular again

C WORK OUT MEANING Read the article carefully and answer the questions. Use the information in the box to help you.

Using contrasts to work out meaning

It's usually possible to work out the meaning of new words and phrases by looking for contrasts with known words and phrases. Look out for linking words (e.g. *while, but*) that signal a contrast.

1 Which underlined adjectives in paragraph 1 mean *old-fashioned*? Which mean *new*?
2 What do the two underlined words in paragraph 2 contrast?
3 What do the underlined words and phrases mean in paragraph 3?
4 What does the underlined phrase in paragraph 4 mean? What is it being contrasted with in the same sentence?
5 Which two verbs are being contrasted in the last sentence in paragraph 4?
6 Which of the underlined words in paragraphs 5 and 6 have a positive meaning? Which have a negative meaning?
7 What do the underlined adjectives in paragraph 7 mean? Which words in the same paragraph have the opposite meanings?

D Work in pairs. Compare your answers to Exercise C.

E SPEAK Work in pairs. Discuss the questions.

1 Do you agree that all successful trends are popular because they fulfill a basic human need?
2 Can you think of any examples or counterexamples to support your opinion?

GRAMMAR

Comparatives and superlatives

A Are these statements true (T) or false (F)?

1 After a comparative adjective (e.g. *bigger*), we always need *than*. *T / F*
2 We form the comparative and superlative of *-ly* adverbs (e.g. *quickly*) by changing *-y* to *-ier*/*-iest*. *T / F*
3 We always need *the* before a superlative (e.g. *fastest*). *T / F*

B Work in pairs. Justify your choices in Exercise A with examples in bold from the *The life cycle of a trend*.

1 ____________
2 ____________
3 ____________

C WORK IT OUT Complete the rules with an example in bold from the article.

Advanced comparatives and superlatives

1 Some modifiers start with *a/an* (e.g. *a little*). When we use these together with *a/an* + noun, the second *a/an* goes after the comparative: ____________
2 Only a few words (*anticipated / expected / hoped for / necessary / usual*) can come between *than* and a noun: ____________
3 We can use the structure *more than* with a small number of verbs (*double, make up for, meet*): ____________

D Go to the **Grammar Hub** on **page VI**.

E SPEAK Tell your partner about one of the following. Use comparative and superlative structures.

- a movie that you enjoyed more than you thought you would
- a concert that you went to or an album you really love
- the most enjoyable vacation you've ever had

SPEAKING

DISCUSS Work in pairs. Compare the following things. Use structures from this lesson.

1 fashion from 1 / 5 / 10 / 20 / 50 years ago
2 popular music from 5 / 10 / 20 / 30 years ago
3 technology now / 10 / 20 / 50 years ago
4 society now / 10 / 20 / 100 years ago

LISTENING

A SPEAK **Work in pairs. Discuss the questions.**

1 What's the difference between the types of people in the box? Do you know any of these types of people?

blogger	influencer	podcaster	trendsetter	vlogger

2 Do you listen to any podcasts or watch any vlogs? If so, which ones?

1.3 **B LISTEN FOR GIST** **Listen to a podcast about trendsetting. Which topics do the speakers give advice about?**

- ☐ 1 making money
- ☐ 2 choosing a focus
- ☐ 3 using social media to build a community
- ☐ 4 the problem with perfection
- ☐ 5 designing your own website
- ☐ 6 learning from statistics
- ☐ 7 long-term planning
- ☐ 8 learning from mistakes

1.3 **C LISTEN FOR DETAIL** **Listen again. Are the statements true (T) or false (F)? Correct the false statements.**

1 Dora and Adam are in the same room. *T / F*
2 Dora regrets that she made so many mistakes. *T / F*
3 Hardly anyone watched Dora's videos at first. *T / F*
4 Dora releases a video at the same time every week. *T / F*
5 Dora replies to every comment on her videos. *T / F*
6 Dora sees herself as an overnight success. *T / F*
7 Adam is unsure about filming himself. *T / F*

D SPEAK **Discuss in pairs.**

1 Do you think the idea of an 'overnight success' is a myth?
2 Have you ever had a blog or vlog? If not, would you ever consider starting one? Why/Why not?

VOCABULARY

Experimenting with prefixes and suffixes

A **Complete Dora's advice using the words in the box.**

amateurish	disaster-prone	hyper-influential	largish	re-editing	super-lucky	tech-savvy	unmute	user-friendly

VLOG AWAY!

A lot of the vlogs on the web are very [1] ______________. Stand out by editing and [2] ______________ until your vlog is as slick and professional as possible.

If you're not particularly [3] ______________, do some research into [4] ______________ software – one with clear instructions.

Look at some of the videos made by the most [5] ______________ vloggers and some with a [6] ______________ number of subscribers. Success isn't down to being [7] ______________, it's about hard work and perfecting the craft.

You don't have to be a [8] ______________ person to sometimes forget to [9] ______________ the mic. Remember not to be too hard on yourself. We all make mistakes, the important thing is to learn from them. You'll get more confident with experience.

B **Complete the information in the box with examples from Exercise A. Use the information in the box to help you.**

Experimenting with prefixes and suffixes

1 Some prefixes (e.g. *un-*, *re-*) allow you to invent completely new verbs: ________, ________
2 *Super-*, *hyper-* and *ultra-* all mean 'much more than usual': ________, ________
3 You can add *-y* or *-ish* to nouns to invent new informal adjectives: *trashy*, *babyish*, ________
4 You can add *-ish* to an adjective or number to mean 'more or less': *twentyish*, *smallish*, ________
5 *Friendly*, *prone*, *proof*, *resistant* and *savvy* can be used as suffixes to make adjectives: *environmentally friendly*, *waterproof*, *heat-resistant*, ________, ________, ________

1.4 **C** **Replace the underlined phrases in these extracts with a word with a prefix or suffix. You may need to change the word order in some sentences. Then listen to check.**

1 You actually need to <u>forget all you learned about</u> all those rules about perfection!
2 Whenever I have a <u>fairly good</u> idea for a podcast, then I try to make it within a few days.
3 You also need to be far more <u>aware of how to use social media</u>.
4 Well, there are plenty of people who post offensive comments <u>that are like spam</u>.
5 Your content would work much better as videos <u>that work well on smartphones</u>.
6 I really think you should <u>think again</u> and become a vlogger instead.
7 I feel <u>incredibly exhausted</u> just thinking about it.

D Go to the **Vocabulary Hub** on **page XVI**.

E **SPEAK** **Work in pairs. Think of examples of the following.**

- websites that aren't very user-friendly / smartphone-friendly
- a person who's tech-savvy / fashion-savvy
- any objects you own that are waterproof or water-resistant
- any objects you own that are damage-prone

PRONUNCIATION
Emphatic stress

1.5 **A** **Listen to the extracts from the recording. Underline the words that are stressed.**

1 One of the most common mistakes that new vloggers and podcasters make is to expect everything to be perfect.
2 But after a while, it got a lot easier!
3 ... if nobody cared after a year, I'd give up. And it did take a while to get noticed.
4 ... you've found your niche and you've created some excellent content.
5 Every Wednesday at ten o'clock, there will be a new video on my channel.
6 I suppose in many people's eyes, I am an overnight success.
7 I felt awkward at first, too, but you do get used to it.
8 Dora Cho, thanks so much for joining me today.

B **Work in pairs. Why did the speaker use emphatic stress in the extracts in Exercise A? Practice saying the sentences.**

1.6 **C** **Decide where to add emphatic stress in these sentences. Then listen to check.**

1 That's one of the most popular vlogs on the web.
2 When you reach one million subscribers, it will be worth it!
3 Is it possible to be a trendsetter and an influencer?

SPEAKING HUB

A **PLAN** **Work in small groups. You are going to make a podcast or vlog episode about trends. Discuss the following questions.**

- What will it be about?
- Why will anyone want to listen/watch?
- What topics could you cover?
- How will you add your own personalities?

B **DISCUSS** **Share your initial ideas with the class. Ask your 'audience' what the next episodes should focus on. Try to engage with them to generate enthusiasm.**

C **PREPARE** **Plan an episode of your podcast/vlog. Don't simply write a script – you'll need to stay spontaneous.**

D **PRESENT** **Make your podcast/vlog. If you have recording equipment, e.g. a phone, you can use that. Otherwise, present your episode to the class.**

Compare different trends
Make a podcast or vlog

1.3 Diet and lifestyle

A *give it a go* **S** using circumlocution

Veganuary

A Work in pairs. You are going to watch a video titled *Veganuary*. What do you think *Veganuary* means?

B Watch the video and check your answers to Exercise A.

C Watch the video again. Complete the sentences with one word or a number.

1. There are now more choices for vegans when they eat out and at ____________.
2. The food which Tabitha says she misses most is ____________.
3. Tabitha initially became a vegan because of ____________ reasons.
4. Many cafés sell a wider selection of products to appeal to ____________.
5. Some people limit eating meat to one or two times a ____________.
6. In the UK ____________ people attempted *Veganuary*.

Glossary

boom (v) to experience an increase in activity, interest or growth
ethics (n) a set of principles that people use to decide what is right and what is wrong
mainstream (adj) considered ordinary or normal and accepted or used by most people
niche (n) a specialized segment of the market for a particular kind of product or service

AUTHENTIC ENGLISH

A Read the sentence from the video. What do you think the phrase in bold means?

Health, ethics, there are just so many reasons, I think, to ***give it a go****.*

B Read the information in the box to check your answer to Exercise A.

give it a go

We use *give it a go* to express it's a good idea to attempt something you haven't done before. We also use *give it a try*, *give it a shot* and *take a stab at it* to express the same idea.

C Work in pairs. Respond to the sentences using *give it a go* or one of the other expressions from the box in Exercise B.

1. We're not sure whether to try skiing when we're in Switzerland.
   Why not give it a shot and see if you like it?
2. Sam would like to study French but he's always found languages difficult.
3. I've never traveled to another country alone before.
4. Nina's always been too shy to introduce herself to complete strangers.

D SPEAK Discuss three things you would like to start doing that you have never tried before.

The big pitch

SAM MALCOLM AMANDA HARRY EMILY

A Watch the video. Work in pairs. Discuss the questions.

1 Who is Sam and how does he spend his day?

2 What do the following people do?

Emily Malcolm Amanda Harry

B Watch the video again. Complete the sentences with the best option.

1 Emily feels *confident about* / *unprepared for* her pitch.

2 Emily would like to *grow her current business* / *start a new sustainable business*.

3 Emily's yoga experience package will include *two* / *three* meals a day.

4 Emily's business will focus on *yoga and food* / *outdoor yoga*.

5 Emily thinks *she will make profits evenly every year* / *her profits will equal her costs in the first year*.

SPEAKING SKILL

A Work in pairs. Look at the example from the video. Why has Emily used this phrase?

Emily: … Well, it's kind of like my yoga classes that I teach, but with the idea that you would be getting more than just exercise.

B Look at the information in the box. Then underline examples of circumlocution in the sentences from the video.

Using circumlocution

We frequently use circumlocution, the use of many words where fewer would do, in a deliberate attempt to be vague or evasive, when we are nervous or can't think of the exact word, or even to make an idea sound more impressive. Look at these other sentences from the video and underline examples of circumlocution.

1 I mean what I really want to do is to expand my business into something more sustainable, you know, a yoga retreat where people can stay for a few days.

2 Full body cleansing, you know the physiological withdrawal of toxins from the body.

C Why do you think Amanda uses circumlocution in the sentences from Exercise B?

D Work in pairs. Ask each other about the following things. When you answer try to be evasive or vague. Use the expressions from Exercise B to help you.

- your favorite café
- your diet
- your job or studies

SPEAKING HUB

A PLAN You are going to make a short pitch for a business you would like to set up. Think of a business idea.

B PREPARE Write notes on what you are going to say. Consider the following points.

- product/service
- USP (Unique Selling Point)
- market
- profitability

C PRESENT Work in groups. Pitch your business idea.

Well, I'd like to give running my own exercise boot camp a try.

D REACT Once everyone in the group has pitched their idea, decide which is the best. Give reasons.

Pitch your own business idea

➤ Turn to page XXIV to learn how to write a blog post about a trend.

Unit 1 Review

GRAMMAR

A Put the words into the correct order to make nominal clauses.

A: Why are you getting rid of those pants? There's nothing wrong with them!

B: Well, the fact [1]**aren't / in the knees / holes / that / there** doesn't mean I can wear them forever. These pants are so last year!

A: Come on! [2] **your clothes / people / think about / what** isn't important! What counts is [3]**on / what's / inside / the!**

B: Exactly! But you know what they say: [4]**on / good / to look / outside / the** is to feel good on the inside. And anyway, [5]**fashion / gives / following** me a lot of pleasure.

A: Yeah, apart from the fact [6]**you can afford / that you spend / more than.**

B: [7]**much / I spend / How** is up to me!

B Choose the correct options (a, b, c or d) to complete each sentence.

1 This is the ___ worst movie I've ever seen.
- a just
- b marginally
- c somewhat
- d absolute

2 There was a slightly larger than ___ crowd at the game.
- a anticipated
- b believed
- c hope for
- d previous

3 Some online stores are ___ as cheap as high-end stores.
- a by far
- b double
- c far and away
- d twice

4 My achievements are ___ as impressive as yours.
- a considerably
- b every bit
- c rather
- d significantly

5 The hotel offers ___ best views across the bay.
- a at least
- b fractionally
- c the very
- d dramatically

VOCABULARY

A Match numbers (1–6) to letters (a–f) to form full sentences.

1 If Jon decides to come to the wedding,
2 If you get a new job in an office,
3 If celebrities dress in a stylish way,
4 If you wear creative and original clothes,
5 If you want to stay cool in the summer,
6 If you're going away for the weekend,

a wear light, baggy clothes.
b you'll fit in well here – everyone has a very unique style.
c pack at least four outfits.
d make sure he doesn't wear his usual scruffy clothes.
e check the company's dress code before you start.
f they usually set a trend.

B Complete the words in the sentences. Some of the letters have been given to help you.

1 I can't afford to eat out again this week – I'm on a very ___ ___ g ___ ___ budget.
2 We offer a range of ___ ___ ___-the-___ ___ ___ ___ and ___ a ___ ___ ___ ___-m ___ ___ ___ suits for our customers.
3 I got really ___ ___ u ___ ___ up this morning when I couldn't find a parking space.
4 I know it seems expensive now, but it's worth it in the long ___ ___ ___.
5 If we are late getting to the store, all the bargains will have been ___ ___ ___ p ___ ___ ___ up!
6 If you have the time to look, you can buy great clothes for p ___ ___ n ___ ___ ___ in thrift stores.
7 The exam was an absolute ___ ___ ___ ___ z ___ – I'm sure I got a great grade!

C Complete the ad using a prefix or suffix from the box with the words in parentheses. Each prefix or suffix may be used more than once. Other changes may be necessary.

-ish ultra- -savvy -prone -y -friendly -proof

TRENDY KID

Are you looking for an [1]________________ (*cool*) fashion gadget for an [2]________________ (*accident*) child?
Our new unbreakable 'Trendy Kid' smartwatch is completely [3]________________ (*child*).

No need to be [4]________________ (*tech*)!
This watch uses the latest skeuomorphic design principles to make it as [5]________________ (*user*) as possible.

Available in [6]________________ (*flower*) pink or [7]________________ (*mud*) brown.

Do you love the design but worry that you'll look too [8]________________ (*child*) wearing a 'Trendy Kid' watch? Head over to our store for a huge range of on-trend adult smartwatches!

2 CREATIVITY

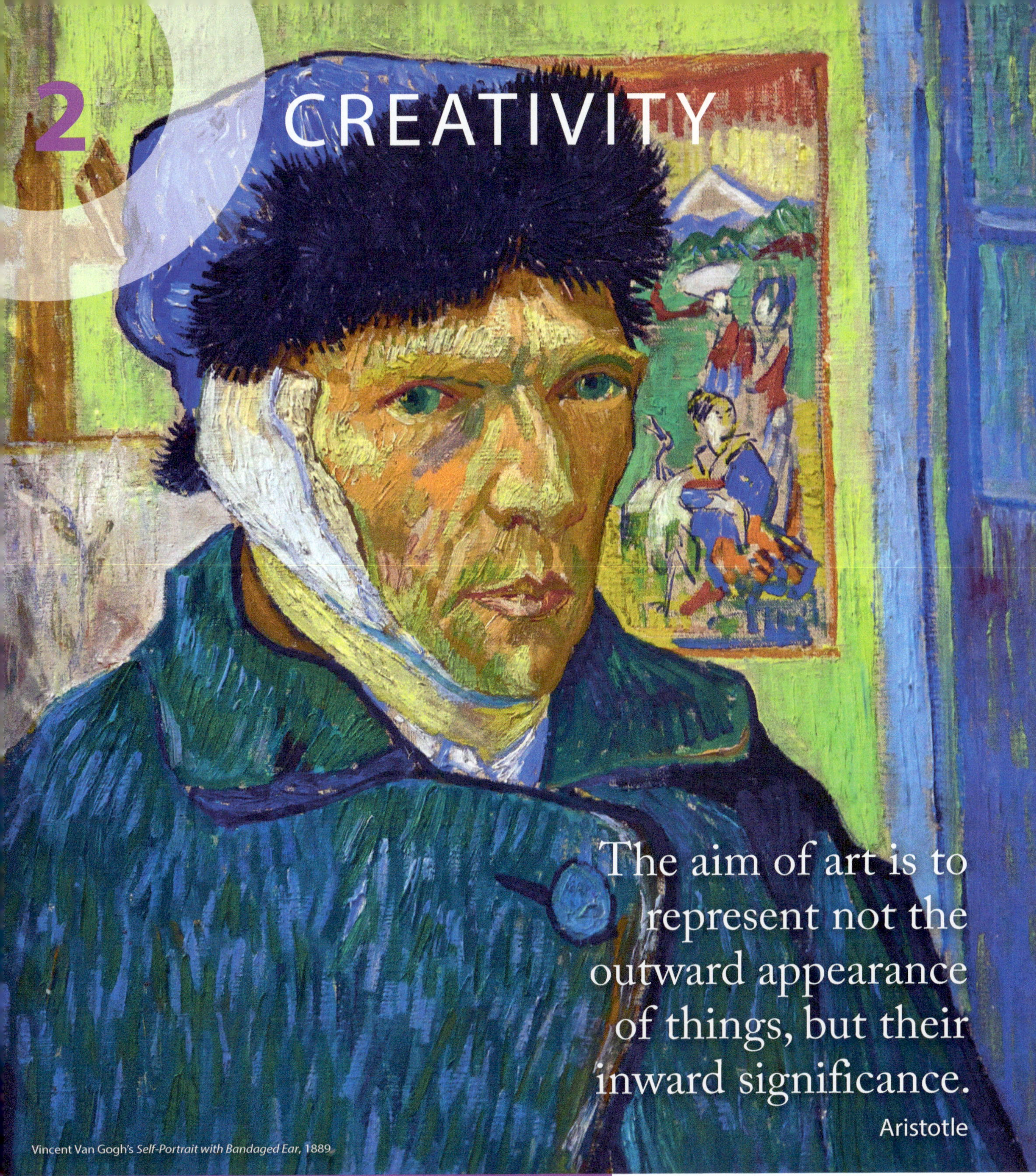

> The aim of art is to represent not the outward appearance of things, but their inward significance.
>
> Aristotle

Vincent Van Gogh's *Self-Portrait with Bandaged Ear*, 1889

OBJECTIVES

- give a presentation about art
- talk about creative projects
- talk about finding inspiration
- describe a life-changing moment
- discuss a work of art
- write a review

Work with a partner. Discuss the questions.

1 Look at the picture. What is your opinion of works of art like this?

2 What does Aristotle mean in the quote? Do you agree with him?

3 Is the main aim, or goal of art:

- to tell a story
- to express emotion
- to persuade
- to celebrate an event
- to create beauty
- to entertain?

2.1 The story behind it

- Give a presentation about art
- Talk about creative projects

V describing art P contrastive stress G narrative tenses S anticipating content before listening

VOCABULARY
Describing art

A SPEAK Work in pairs. Look at the pictures (a–e) and discuss the questions.

1 Do you know any of these works of art?

2 Which do you prefer? Why?

B Choose the correct adjectives to complete the comments (1–5).

C Go to the **Vocabulary Hub** on **page XVI**.

D What art forms are being described in Exercise B?

1 ________ 2 ________ 3 ________ 4 ________ 5 ________

E SPEAK Think of an example of an art form from Exercise D. Describe it to your partner.

I find this installation groundbreaking. It makes you think about space in a different way.
It's actually fairly … It's not that … It's somewhat …

1 I think some famous works of art are ***overrated / repetitive***. But that isn't the case here. The artist's use of light and shade in this composition was different from anything that had come before – it was truly ***pretentious / groundbreaking***.

2 It was ***hilarious / tedious***! I couldn't stop laughing. OK, the same jokes again and again become a little ***underrated / repetitive***, but the comic performances were ***awesome / appalling***.

3 It's a very ***unconventional / repetitive*** piece. I can see why some people wouldn't want something so big and strange put up in a public space. They probably think it's a little ***acclaimed / pretentious***, as if the artist is trying too hard to be different.

4 Most people recognize this image. It's so ***iconic / hilarious***, capturing the mood of the time it was taken. It's ***thought-provoking / unconventional***, too – it really makes you consider the human story behind this historical event.

5 The risk with performances like this is if the songs are ***appalling / iconic*** then it's really not enjoyable. It just makes them really ***tedious / awesome*** – so long and slow. Fortunately the music, lighting and costumes in this show were really special. It was a truly ***sensational / iconic*** experience. I can see why it's been ***overrated / acclaimed*** by critics and audiences.

a

b

LISTENING

A Work in pairs. Read a review of the radio show *More than meets the eye*. Are there similar radio shows in your country?

> ### *More than meets the eye*
>
> gives an analysis of one different piece of groundbreaking fine art each week. The guest speakers make these discussions unique and sometimes fairly unconventional. They don't just have specialist knowledge of the artist, but also some personal connection to the pieces.

B **ANTICIPATE CONTENT** You're going to listen to an episode of *More than meets the eye* about picture b. Work in pairs and answer the questions below. Use the information in the box to help you.

> **Anticipating content before listening**
>
> You can use different types of information to predict what you will hear.
>
> - Read notes, reviews, handouts, etc.
> - Look at titles or images for clues about what the speaker will cover.
> - Use your own knowledge to predict topics or themes.
> - Use information to think of questions you expect to be answered.

1 What topics will be discussed in the show?

____

2 What questions will be answered?

____

2.1 **C** **LISTEN FOR GIST** Listen to the show and check your predictions in Exercise B.

2.2 **D** **LISTEN FOR DETAIL** Listen and write down the different ideas about who the main subject of the painting is.

1 ______________________

2 ______________________

3 ______________________

E **SPEAK** Work in pairs and discuss the questions.

1 Who do you think the subject of the painting is?

2 Why do you think the artist chose this composition?

PRONUNCIATION

Contrastive stress

2.3 **A** Listen to these extracts from the radio show. Draw arrows to show whether the intonation rises (↗) or falls (↘).

1 Yes, we can see her entourage on the right (__), but to the left (__), we can see the artist himself, standing next to a gigantic canvas.

2 So, it's a portrait of the King and Queen (__), not the Infanta (__).

2.4 **B** Underline the words you think will be stressed and draw arrows to show where you think the intonation will rise (↗) or fall (↘). Then listen to check.

1 Actually, Mondrian wasn't American, he was Dutch.

2 Although I like his landscapes, his portraits are much better.

3 Why don't we watch a movie instead of going to the gallery?

4 I don't think it's tedious. I just think it's overrated.

5 It was painted in 1656 – you said 1666.

6 **A:** You study art history, don't you?

B: No, I study fine art, not art history.

C **SPEAK** Guess whether your partner likes these things or not. Respond to your partner's guesses. Use contrastive stress when appropriate.

> classical music   comic books   crime novels
> heavy metal   Hollywood movies   modern art   musicals
> science fiction movies   soap operas

A: You like Spider-Man comicbooks.
B: No, I like Batman not Spider-Man.

SPEAKING

A Choose a work of art that you really like. It could be a painting, a sculpture, a photograph, a movie, a book, a play, a poem or a song.

B **PLAN** Write notes so that you can talk about:

- information about the artist / writer / singer
- a description of the work of art
- your interpretation of the work of art
- the reasons why you like this work of art.

C **PRESENT** Give a short presentation to your partner about the work of art you have chosen.

D **DISCUSS** Ask your partner about the work of art he or she chose.

c

d

e

READING

A PREDICT Look at the pictures in the article. What kind of place is this? Do you know anything about it?

B SKIM Read the box below about the Eden Project. Check your answers to Exercise A.

C READ FOR DETAIL Read *How we made the Eden Project*. Put the events (a–h) in the correct order. Two events are not needed.

___ **a** They hired a lot of people to work on the project.
___ **b** They did a lot of tests to make sure the building would be safe.
___ **c** They tried out some innovative techniques.
___ **d** They had to stop working until they found more money.
___ **e** They started working on designs without a specific location in mind.
___ **f** Tim Smit had the inspiration for the project.
___ **g** They found the ideal location.
___ **h** They conducted a feasibility study.

The Eden Project is a spectacular tropical garden housed inside huge plastic bubbles within a crater the size of thirty soccer fields.

How we made the Eden Project

Tim Smit, *founder*

We started the construction with just $3000 in the bank. To persuade government officials to part with public funds, you have to do a feasibility study and that's expensive. So we simply progressed on faith, and hope, promising ourselves that we'd never use the word *if* only *when*.

The idea for a huge horticultural expo had come to me as I worked on the Lost Gardens of Heligan. [1]I'd always loved the thought of a lost civilization in a volcanic crater, and when I saw the lunar landscape of the old Cornish clay pits, [2]I realized they'd be the perfect site.

A friend put me in touch with an architecture firm. I hadn't received a penny in funding at that point, or even a site, just a belief that the idea of a lost world in a crater would appeal to anyone who's ever been 12. They thought the idea was crazy, but it struck them as an adventure and they agreed to start work for nothing. Meanwhile, a construction firm put some money into the project in return for a share of the profits. Everyone was now suddenly highly motivated.

Our two horticultural directors recruited anyone they'd ever worked with and debated what to put in the buildings. I'd envisaged rainforest and Mediterranean areas, eager for it to be the greatest ever collection of plants useful to humans. But it was also a question of finding a balance between the wow factor and more meditative moments. So we have a giant waterfall along with a prairie that, in the winter, is about the most boring thing you can see – then, for six weeks a year, it bursts into spectacular life.

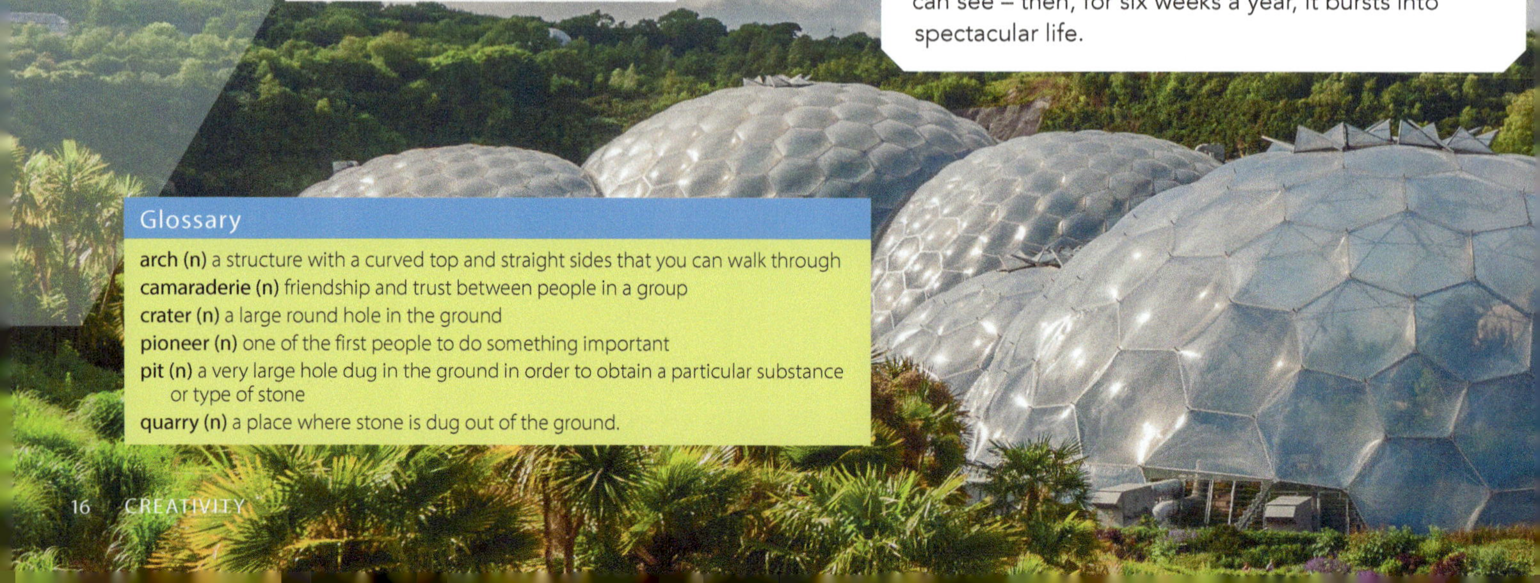

Glossary

arch (n) a structure with a curved top and straight sides that you can walk through
camaraderie (n) friendship and trust between people in a group
crater (n) a large round hole in the ground
pioneer (n) one of the first people to do something important
pit (n) a very large hole dug in the ground in order to obtain a particular substance or type of stone
quarry (n) a place where stone is dug out of the ground.

D SCAN Read the article again. What were the obstacles they had to overcome to build the Eden Project?

E SPEAK Work in pairs. Discuss the questions.

1 Why do you think people agreed to work on the project while funding was uncertain?
2 Why do you think this project succeeded?
3 Would you like to have worked on this project?
4 What other kinds of projects would you like to work on?

Jolyon Brewis, *architect of Grimshaw Architects*

Most architects dream of creating a new world on a scale that eclipses all that's gone before. So, in the early days, when there was always the threat of construction being stopped because of lack of money, all the companies involved carried on regardless: we were so enthralled by the vision.

Our first designs were for different locations, including a tent-like structure for a hillside, then Smit discovered the china clay quarry at Bodelva. It had a romantic, lost world feel since it would be hidden from view until you were almost upon it. For a long while it all seemed like a terrific gamble. Usually, the one thing an architect can rely on is solid ground, but since it was still a working quarry there was a lot of movement. What's more, to figure out costs, we had to design our buildings right down to the last detail, even though no one knew if there'd even be enough money to buy the site.

[3]We'd been working on a series of snaking arches linked with glass, but while one of our design teams [4]were cleaning up, they realized that bubbles would have far more stability on the shifting soil. Building on such a huge scale involved untried technology: this was a leap into the unknown. Glass would have been too heavy so we pioneered 11-meter hexagonal pillows of inflated plastic. It had never been used so big before and we had no idea how it would behave. So we had to work through various disaster scenarios, such as what would happen if one deflated, then filled up with water and brought down the entire structure.

The worst moments were at the beginning when we [5]hadn't been given the funding yet and some of the foundations [6]got washed away during one of the wettest winters in memory. But there was a great feeling of camaraderie. We felt there was nothing we couldn't cope with.

GRAMMAR
Narrative tenses

A Match the underlined words (1–6) in the article with the tenses.

simple past	___	past perfect progressive	___
past progressive	___	simple past passive voice	___
past perfect	___	past perfect passive voice	___

B WORK IT OUT Complete the rules with the tenses in Exercise A.

Narrative tenses

1 When we tell a story, we use the ______________ and ______________ to explain the main events.
2 We use the ______________ and ______________ to give background information for actions that were completed before the main events of the story.
3 We use the ______________ and ______________ to give background information for actions that were in progress before the main events of the story.

C Go to the **Grammar Hub** on **page VIII**.

D Choose a sentence and continue the story. (It doesn't have to be a true story!)

1 I had been working for several hours when …
2 I had been planning to go to … for months, but …
3 I had just gone to bed when …
4 It had been raining all day, so …
5 I had been feeling sick all day because …
6 I had already eaten a big breakfast, but …

SPEAKING HUB

A PREPARE Think of an anecdote about an interesting project you worked on or a piece of work you have done. Use the ideas below to help you prepare what you are going to say.

- what was the project or piece of work
- what went well
- what went badly
- what would you do differently if you could do it again

B PRESENT Work in groups. Tell your anecdote about the project or piece of work.

C DISCUSS Listen to your classmates' anecdotes, react to what they say and ask questions.

D REFLECT Choose the best anecdotes.

Give a presentation about art
Talk about creative projects

2.2 Creative people

- Talk about finding inspiration
- Describe a life-changing moment

V – ideas and inspiration; compound adjectives
P – questions for comment or criticism
G – future in the past
S – inferring meaning

VOCABULARY
Ideas and inspiration

A Read the blog post *Sparking ideas*. Choose the correct definition (a or b) for the underlined phrases (1–10).

1 **a** find the right location
b find the right mood

2 **a** abandon an idea
b develop an idea

3 **a** working from nothing
b working with no equipment

4 **a** steal someone's ideas
b discuss something with someone

5 **a** get ideas from
b paint a picture of

6 **a** escape a problem
b help you to think of some ideas

7 **a** become very involved with something
b are about to finish

8 **a** feel more energetic about
b get a different view of

9 **a** find a good idea
b am unable to progress

10 **a** think carefully
b rely on your feelings

SPARKING IDEAS

Jasmine, artist

'Some people are very practical about finding ideas. But not me. I need to [1]get into the right state of mind, whatever it takes. It means traveling miles to get away from everyone, working through the night or going for a walk – until I find inspiration or it finds me. Then I just [2]run with an idea and see where it takes me.'

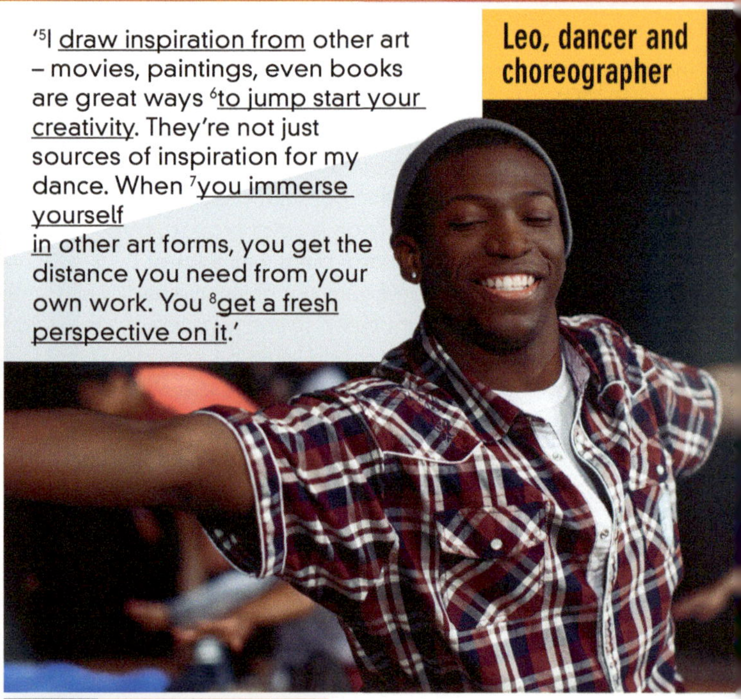

Leo, dancer and choreographer

'[5]I draw inspiration from other art – movies, paintings, even books are great ways [6]to jump start your creativity. They're not just sources of inspiration for my dance. When [7]you immerse yourself in other art forms, you get the distance you need from your own work. You [8]get a fresh perspective on it.'

Michelle, director

'[3]Working from a blank canvas, with no idea where you are going to start, can be really scary. So, … I call my mom! It's great [4]to bounce ideas off someone. Even if you disagree, it can help you move forward.'

Sam, playwright

'Although writing is my job, when [9]I hit a wall and just can't find the ideas, I start doodling cartoons, shapes. It really helps me to think. Then when the ideas start to come, [10]you trust your instincts. You just know which ideas to use, which to combine and which to just forget.'

B Choose the correct phrases to complete the sentences.

1 I've just *gotten into the right state of mind / hit a wall* with this project. I have no inspiration and can't get any further with it.

2 With art projects, you can't always know for certain you have the best idea. Sometimes you just have to *trust your instincts / work from a blank canvas*.

3 When you're feeling uninspired, talk to other people. *Bouncing ideas off someone / Running with an idea* can only help.

4 When there are no distractions and you are completely focused, you can truly *get a fresh perspective on / immerse yourself in* something.

5 We had no idea where we could begin with the design. We were *jump starting our creativity / working from a blank canvas*.

C SPEAK Work in pairs. Do you ever have to be creative in your daily life? How do you come up with ideas?

LISTENING

2.5 **A** LISTEN FOR MAIN IDEA Listen to Mark and Lauren discussing an article about inspiration. What seven tips for getting inspiration do they discuss?

SEVEN TIPS FOR GETTING INSPIRATION

1 ______
2 ______
3 ______
4 ______
5 ______
6 ______
7 ______

2.5 **B** LISTEN FOR DETAIL Listen again. Which of the tips does Mark like?

C SPEAK Work in pairs. Have you ever tried any of the ideas mentioned in Exercise A? Why/Why not?

PRONUNCIATION

Questions for comment or criticism

2.6 **A** Listen to the questions from the discussion. Draw arrows in the parentheses to show whether the intonation rises (↗) or falls (↘) at the end of each sentence.

1 Isn't that somewhat pretentious? ( )
2 Is he crazy? ( )
3 Why does she keep writing if it's terrible? ( )
4 Don't you think? ( )
5 Is she serious? ( )
6 How can you make something when you don't know what you're doing? ( )

2.7 **B** Choose the correct intonation for the questions. Then listen to check your answers.

1 **A:** Do you think it's sensible to schedule time for creativity?
B: What's the point of that? (*rise / fall*) You can't be creative if you're not in the right state of mind.

2 **A:** Do you ever have creative ideas while you're dreaming?
B: Yes, but I can never remember them. Isn't that frustrating? (*rise / fall*)

3 **A:** Do you find it easier to be creative when you're listening to music?
B: Are you serious? (*rise / fall*) I can't think properly unless it's quiet.

4 **A:** Do you feel more creative early in the morning or late at night?
B: Late at night. Definitely. Who feels creative first thing in the morning? (*rise / fall*)

C SPEAK Ask your partner the questions in Exercise B. Try to use a question for comment or criticism in your answer.

SPEAKING

A Look at the infographic. Think of an advantage and disadvantage for each suggestion.

B Work in pairs. Compare your ideas with your partner.

C Now decide which is the best suggestion for finding ideas. Talk for about one minute.

D DISCUSS Work in pairs and discuss the questions.

1 Are you a creative person?
2 How important is the ability to be creative?
3 Do you think everyone should try to do something creative from time to time?

VOCABULARY
Compound adjectives

A Complete the fame quiz.

ARE YOU CUT OUT FOR FAME?

RATE YOURSELF ON A SCALE OF 1 to 5.
1 = Strongly agree 5 = Strongly disagree

1. You would trade having privacy for being world famous. 1 2 3 4 5
2. You are very focused on one kind of career. You are not open-minded to other career choices. 1 2 3 4 5
3. You would describe yourself as a highly-motivated person. 1 2 3 4 5
4. You are thick skinned. You don't mind being criticized. 1 2 3 4 5
5. You would rather be self-employed than do part-time work for someone else for the same money. 1 2 3 4 5
6. You'd prefer to be paid less in a fun creative job than well paid and bored at work. 1 2 3 4 5
7. You can handle working long days and doing late-night shifts. 1 2 3 4 5

B Work in pairs. Turn to page XX of the Communication Hub to see what your answers say about you.

C Find eight compound adjectives in the quiz. Use the information in the box to help you.

Compound adjectives

Compound adjectives can be formed in several ways, including:

- adjective + noun: *last-minute*
- adjective + participle: *left-handed*
- adverb + participle: *never-ending*
- noun + adjective: *sun-dried*
- noun + participle: *career-ending*

We always hyphenate compound adjectives before a noun, but not after a noun. However, some compound adjectives are written as one word (e.g. *heartwarming*) or always hyphenated (e.g. *self-important*).

D Go to the Vocabulary Hub on page XVII.

E **SPEAK** Work in pairs and discuss the questions. Use some of the adjectives in Exercise C.

1 Would you like to be famous?

2 What do you think are the good and bad points of being famous?

CHANGE OF PLANS

Some people choose a career at a young age and stick with it. However, here are four famous people who ended up with very different careers from what they expected.

CHARLIZE THERON

Charlize Theron, originally from South Africa, was to have been a ballerina. However, she suffered a career-ending injury to her knee that meant she had to abandon her childhood dream. Instead, she decided she would turn to acting. After finding it difficult to land speaking roles, she watched hours of television to try to pick up an American accent. But, the roles still didn't come and although she was getting modeling work, money was tight. One day she was trying to cash a check at the bank but the teller said he was not going to accept it. Theron started to argue with the teller, making a scene in the bank as she tried to explain that she was about to be thrown out of her apartment if she couldn't cash the check. Eventually a man in the line behind her came over to help resolve the situation and, after she had her money, he gave her his business card – he was an agent. A couple of months later, Theron had landed her first movie role.

ANDREA BOCELLI

World-famous opera singer Andrea Bocelli was supposed to have a very different career. Although he displayed a clear talent for music from an early age, his parents encouraged him to study law so that he would always have a steady income. Following his parents' advice, he attended law school and became a lawyer. However, he also continued with his music – playing in piano bars in the evenings to earn money for singing lessons. It was at one of these bars where he got the lucky break that was to launch his career. Zucchero, a famous Italian singer, heard him sing, and thought that he would be perfect for a demo he wanted to make. As a result of that meeting, Bocelli ending up going on tour with Zucchero. Bocelli even sang at Zucchero's birthday party – and was immediately signed up by an agent at the party. The agent knew he was going to be a big star – and she was right.

Glossary

renovate (v) to make something old look new again by repairing and improving it, especially a building

embroidery (n) the activity of decorating cloth with colored stitches

READING

A SPEAK Look at the pictures of the people in the article *Change of plans*. What do you know about them?

B READ FOR DETAIL Read *Change of plans*. What do the four people's stories have in common?

C INFER MEANING Read the article again and answer the questions. Use the information in the box to help you.

Inferring meaning

Writers do not always explain everything in detail. They sometimes provide readers with the facts and allow them to infer the meaning by drawing a conclusion from the available information.

1 Why was Charlize Theron unable to get speaking roles?

2 Does Andrea Bocelli still work as a lawyer?

3 What do we know about Harrison Ford's personality when he was younger?

4 How did Grandma Moses learn to paint?

D SPEAK Work in pairs and discuss the questions

1 Which was the most interesting story? Why?

2 Which person do you think was the luckiest?

HARRISON FORD

Harrison Ford first became interested in acting at the age of 18 because he thought it would be an easy way to get a good grade on his English course. He dropped out of college and moved to Hollywood in his early 20s. He managed to get some small acting jobs, but after a few years he became frustrated with the kind of roles he was being offered. While renovating his house, he decided to use the tools he had bought and the skills he had learned to become a self-employed carpenter. One day, movie director George Lucas hired Ford to make some cabinets for his home and after meeting him, decided to cast him in a movie he was making called *American Graffiti*. When Lucas was auditioning actors for his next movie, he was one actor short so he asked Ford to help out. In the end, he cast Ford and the movie, *Star Wars*, would go on to become a huge hit and make Ford a star.

GRANDMA MOSES

Grandma Moses (Anna Mary Robertson Moses) became a famous painter at the age of 80 – despite not having had any formal training. She was born in 1860 and raised on her parents' farm. She didn't attend school regularly, because she knew she would be leaving home to start working on another farm when she was 12. She married at 17, was widowed at 47, and retired at 76. In fact, she didn't start painting until she took it up as a hobby at the age of 78. She only started because she was giving up embroidery due to pain from arthritis. She painted rural scenes from her childhood, which she gave away or sold cheaply. However, one day an art collector saw her paintings in a local store. He drove straight to her farm and asked to buy all the paintings she had, and, later that year, he exhibited some of her paintings at a show for new painters. This led to solo exhibitions, and soon her shows would break attendance records around the world. She died in 1961.

GRAMMAR

Future in the past

A WORK IT OUT Look at the underlined phrases in the article. Then choose the correct words to complete the rules.

Future in the past

1 When we talk about plans, intentions and predictions that we had in the past, we use ***past / present*** forms of the verbs we usually use to talk about the future.

2 We use *be* + *to* + base form for events that ***came true / didn't come true*** and *be* + *to* + *have* + past participle (or *be* + *supposed to* + verb) for events that ***came true / didn't come true***.

B Go to the **Grammar Hub** on **page VIII**.

C Write sentences using the future in the past to explain the situations (1–5). Then share your ideas with a partner.

1 You didn't get up early today.

2 You missed your train or bus this morning.

3 You didn't eat lunch yesterday.

4 You got lost in the city.

5 You went to see a movie with a friend.

I was going to get up early, but I forgot to set my alarm clock.

SPEAKING HUB

A PLAN Think of a time when a change of plans had a big effect on your life. Choose one of these situations or think of your own idea.

- You changed your mind about something.
- You suddenly had an unexpected opportunity.
- Something did not go as you had planned.
- Something good came out of a bad situation.

B PREPARE Write notes to prepare to talk about this event.

C PRESENT Tell your partner about what happened.

D DISCUSS Listen and ask your partner questions.

- Talk about finding inspiration
- Describe a life-changing moment

Café Hub

2.3 Art and design

A– *nowhere* phrases   S– managing a discussion

City design festival

a

b

A Work in pairs. Look at the pictures (a and b) and discuss the questions.

1 Where are they?

2 What do you think they are?

B Watch the video and check your answers to Exercise A.

Glossary

accessible (adj) art, music, literature, etc, which is easy to understand and enjoy

ceramic (adj) made from clay baked at a high temperature so that it has become hard

eccentricity (n) the state of behaving in a strange and unusual way, sometimes in a humorous way

installation (n) a piece of art that consists of several objects or pictures arranged to produce a particular effect

C Watch the video again. Check (✓) the things you see.

1 People walking inside an installation. ☐

2 A designer creating an installation. ☐

3 An indoor design exhibition. ☐

4 A man sitting at a table with a cup of coffee. ☐

5 Children playing on the installation. ☐

6 A person taking a photo of an installation. ☐

7 People walking through arches. ☐

8 A designer showing a group of people around an installation. ☐

D Watch the video again. Complete the sentences with the best option.

1 What Camille Walala loves most about an outdoor art installation is that it *makes art easier for people to understand and enjoy / allows her to be more creative*.

2 Camille has lived in London for *fifteen / twenty* years.

3 A woman says Camille Walala's installation looks like a *theme park / bouncy castle*.

4 Adam Nathaniel Furman says people think ceramics are something *found in your bathroom and kitchen / used to cover buildings*.

5 Ben Evans says *a minority / the majority* of London's design community have British passports.

AUTHENTIC ENGLISH

A Work in pairs. Read the sentences from the video. Then choose the correct words to complete the information in the box.

*There's **nowhere quite like** it, especially when it comes to design.*

*I absolutely love London, it's like an eccentricity that you've got **nowhere else**.*

***There's nowhere else** really in the UK where you can just walk down the street and see exciting things like this every day.*

nowhere phrases

We use *there's nowhere quite like, that you've got nowhere else* and *there's nowhere else where* to express that a place is ***ordinary / unique***.

We have many other phrases with *nowhere like: nowhere on Earth, ... but nowhere more so than ..., out of nowhere, go nowhere, be going nowhere fast, in the middle of nowhere, nowhere near* and *nowhere to be found*.

B Write sentences using phrases with *nowhere* about these places.

1 Paris *There's nowhere on earth like Paris for culture.*

2 London ____________________

3 Dubai ____________________

4 New York ____________________

5 Italy ____________________

6 Brazil ____________________

C Work in pairs. Tell each other about some of your favorite places (countries, cities, restaurants, stores, museums, etc) and why they are unique.

Art critics

SAM MALCOLM AMANDA HARRY EMILY

A Work in pairs. Discuss the questions.

1 Do you like modern art? Why/Why not?
2 What do you think about art criticism?

B Watch the video and answer the questions.

1 What does Malcolm like about the painted paper?
2 What does each of the following people think the message of the painted paper is?
   - Amanda
   - Malcolm
   - male customer
3 Whose opinion is most popular among the three of them?
4 What misunderstanding has occurred?

SPEAKING SKILL

A Work in pairs. Look at the underlined expression from the video and answer the questions.

Amanda: The artist is clearly making a comment on …
Sam: I think you're a little confused …
Amanda: Sam … <u>Can you let me finish?</u> Thanks. The artist is clearly making a statement on feelings of isolation …

1 What has happened in the exchange between Sam and Amanda?
2 Why do we use expressions like this when we're speaking?

Read the information in the box. Which of the ways of managing a discussion (1–5) are used in the exchange in Exercise A?

B Match the ways of managing a discussion (1–5) with the examples from the video (a–e) below.

Managing a discussion

1 Interrupting: Say something to stop someone speaking so that you can speak instead.
2 Taking the floor: Signal that you are now going to join a debate or discussion.
3 Returning to a point: Indicate that you want to further discuss a point that you previously made.
4 Stopping an interruption: Tell the person who is trying to interrupt that you want to finish your point first.
5 Pre-empting an interruption: Anticipate that someone will interrupt you and briefly state all the points you want to cover before they cut in.

a Well that leads back to my point … without meaning there is no relationship.
b If I could just finish … my main point though is that it doesn't really matter what it is.
c I couldn't agree more … it does evoke some really intense emotions.
d I don't mean to cut you off, Amanda, but I think it's the exact opposite.
e And that's my point exactly. When you are using bold colors like this artist has, you are clearly trying to expose just how superficial those connections are.

C Work in small groups. Discuss one of the following topics. Use the strategies from Exercise B.

- Art in the past and now
- The greatest artist ever
- Different forms of art

SPEAKING HUB

A PREPARE You are going to talk about a work of art in a small group. Look at the picture on page 13. Think about what you want to say about the picture and art in general.

B PRESENT Work in small groups. Discuss the picture and present your views.

A: I usually tend to prefer landscapes rather than portraits …
B: Can I just stop you there? … The style of painting is what makes it special.
A: Exactly. What I was actually saying was that while I usually prefer landscapes, in this case …

Discuss a work of art

➤ Turn to page XXV to learn how to write a review about a classic book or movie.

Unit 2 Review

VOCABULARY

A **Complete the conversations with the words in the box.**

groundbreaking hilarious repetitive
sensational tedious unconventional

1 **A:** That was a really funny movie. I was crying with laughter.
B: Yes, it was ______________.

2 **A:** I thought her performance was amazing.
B: She was ______________. She deserves an Oscar.

3 **A:** Have you read this book? I'm finding it pretty dull.
B: Yeah, it's a little ______________, isn't it?

4 **A:** It was such an innovative musical. I loved it.
B: Me, too. As you say, it was ______________.

5 **A:** Can we turn this off? It's just car chase after car chase.
B: Yeah, it's kind of ______________, isn't it?

6 **A:** Do you like her work? Her pieces are very unusual.
B: She's ______________, but I find her work exciting.

B **Complete the sentences with the words in the box. Then choose which ideas help you feel most creative.**

bounce draw fresh trust
immerse run stimulate hit

1 Take a break. ______________ yourself in a TV show for 30 minutes.
2 ______________ ideas around with your best friend. Ask them for a ______________ perspective.
3 ______________ inspiration from a piece of music.
4 Whenever you ______________ a wall, take a walk.
5 Drink coffee to ______________ your creativity.
6 Don't think carefully – just ______________ with an idea. ______________ your instincts.

C **Match numbers (1–8) to letters (a–h) to form full sentences. Then think of some jobs which match each sentence.**

1 You need to be thick-
2 It's a well-
3 You need to be highly
4 Most people won't become world-
5 It's like being self-
6 There are a lot of late-
7 You have to be open-
8 It's a high-

a night shifts, so you'll have an irregular sleeping pattern.
b risk job, so it pays well.
c employed, because you can work from home.
d paid job.
e minded, because things change all the time.
f motivated, because it's competitive.
g skinned to handle the criticism.
h famous, but they still make a living.

GRAMMAR

A **Complete the text with the correct form of the verbs in parentheses.**

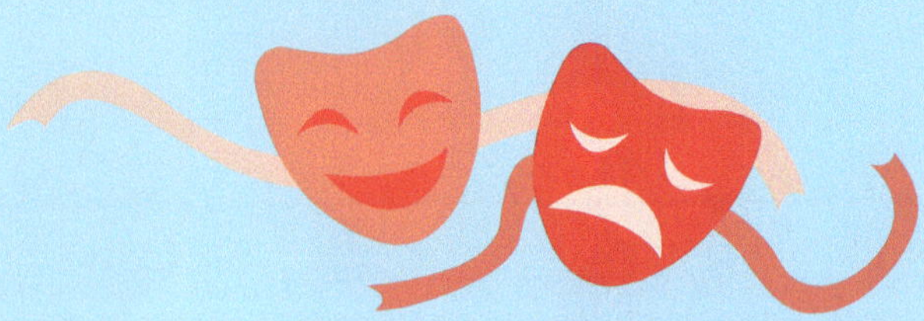

My first role

When I was about ten, I [1] ______________ (*join*) a drama group in a nearby town and they [2] ______________ (*perform*) a show every year. That year, we [3] ______________ (*do*) *Peter Pan*.

We [4] ______________ (*rehearse*) for weeks. I [5] ______________ (*give*) a pretty big role – I [6] ______________ (*play*) Michael, the smallest of the children Peter Pan [7] ______________ (*bring*) to Neverland. I [8] ______________ (*remember*) how nervous I [9] ______________ (*be*) when we [10] ______________ (*peek*) out from behind the curtain to see the people in the audience.

However, it was worth all the nerves when the audience [11] ______________ (*applaud*) at the end. I [12] ______________ (*feel*) so proud – and I couldn't wait to start practicing for the next show.

B **Choose the correct option to complete the sentences.**

1 The band did not know they ***would have / were going to be*** the biggest selling rock group this decade.
2 Little did he know, it was this discovery that ***would change / is to have changed*** the experiment completely.
3 This ***was supposed to be / would be*** a dream vacation, but it turned into a nightmare.
4 They ***were supposed to finish / be finished*** in May, but the deadline was pushed back until June.
5 The highway was ***due / meant*** to be completed by now.
6 Carlos had been ***about / set*** to go through airport security when he realized he didn't have his passport.

3 PROGRESS

> If there is no struggle, there is no progress.
>
> Frederick Douglass

Blazing a trail at thirty thousand feet.

OBJECTIVES

- make predictions about the future
- use persuasive language to sell something
- discuss progress and society
- evaluate costs and benefits
- discuss renewable energy
- write a persuasive email

Work with a partner. Discuss the questions.

1 Look at the picture. What does it say about progress? What other examples can you think of to illustrate the same idea?

2 Read the quote. What does Douglass mean?

3 How could you measure 'progress':

- in your own life
- in your city/country
- in the world?

3.1 Progressive design

- Make predictions about the future
- Use persuasive language to sell something

V – sustainability; forming verbs from adjectives
P – sounding persuasive
G – future structures
S – listening to identify persuasive techniques

VOCABULARY
Sustainability

A Work in groups. Which of these sustainable / environmentally friendly solutions would most benefit your country?

- recycling
- biodegradable plastic
- electric vehicles
- beach clean-ups
- wind power

B Choose the correct words to complete these statements about sustainability.

1 We will *never* / *soon* run out of **renewable** energy sources like solar and wind power.
2 A sustainable building generates *less* / *more* electricity than it **consumes**.
3 To be carbon-**neutral**, you might *cut down* / *plant* some trees to **offset** the pollution caused by a plane trip.
4 A zero-**emission** factory causes no *air* / *water* pollution.
5 **Over-exploitation** of natural resources will *lead to* / *prevent* the **depletion** of those resources over time.
6 **Biodegradable** materials break down into *harmful* / *harmless* parts which don't **accumulate** in the environment.

C Go to the Vocabulary Hub on page XVII.

D SPEAK Work in groups. Discuss the questions.

1 Can ordinary people be carbon-neutral/cause zero emissions in the modern world?
2 Is it worth the effort? Can ordinary people make a difference?

READING

A SPEAK Look at the pictures in the article. What might be special or unusual about the buildings?

B READ FOR GIST Read the article quickly. Match the names below with the pictures (a–c).

1 Aequorea ___
2 Nautilus Eco-Resort ___
3 The Lilypad ___

C READ FOR DETAIL Read the article again. Which project(s) from Exercise B does each statement apply to?

1 Scientists will work there.
2 It takes its shape from the natural world.
3 It will collect its own water.
4 It will use less energy than it generates.
5 The buildings will move up and down.
6 It will move from place to place.
7 It will hold tens of thousands of people.

D SPEAK Would you like to live or stay in any of these places? What would be the benefits and drawbacks?

a

GRAMMAR
Future structures

A Look at the underlined sections (1–10) in the article. What time do they refer to?

B WORK IT OUT Match the sections (1–10) with the rules in the box (a–f).

Future structures

a We use the future progressive to describe a situation that will be in progress at a particular point in the future (__), or to emphasize that it will cover an extended period of time (__).

b We use the future perfect to describe changes that will be completed before a particular point in the future (__).

c We use the future perfect progressive to focus on the future results of an earlier future process, and/or to measure the length of time of that process (__).

d We can use a modal verb (e.g. *might*, *could*) instead of *will* in these structures (__).

e After words like *if*, *unless*, *when*, *while*, etc, future tenses (e.g. future progressive) usually become present tenses (e.g. present progressive) (__, __).

f Other future structures include *be on the brink/verge of (doing)* (__) and *be about / due / set to (do)* (__, __).

C Go to the Grammar Hub on page X.

SPEAKING

SPEAK Work in pairs. Ask and answer the questions about the times in the box.

ten years from now	the end of this lesson	this time next year

1 Where will you be? What will you be doing?
2 What will you have achieved? How will the world have changed?
3 How will you be feeling? Why?

ONE ARCHITECT'S VISION

TO BRING US BACK FROM THE BRINK

The world of 2100 will look considerably different from the world of today. [1]By then, much of the ice around the north and south poles will have melted, according to the Intergovernmental Panel on Climate Change. [2]Sea levels could well have risen by as much as 88 cm. [3]Many of the world's low-lying islands and coastal regions will be disappearing – or will already have disappeared – beneath the rising tides. Millions of people will have lost their homes. In short, [4]we're on the brink of witnessing irrevocable changes to our world.

A visionary Belgian architect, Vincent Callebaut, has an innovative answer to the problem of rising sea levels: The Lilypad, a futuristic-looking city that will drift around the world following ocean currents like a giant ship. If his plans come to fruition, [5]this self-contained city is set to become home to around 50,000 climate refugees.

The Lilypad's design is inspired by the shape of the *Victoria amazonica* lilypad. At its center will be a lake to catch, store and purify rain water, surrounded by three 'mountains'. Thanks to a series of renewable energy sources, this eco-city will produce more energy than it consumes. All its carbon dioxide and other waste will be recycled, making the Lilypad entirely zero-emission.

The Lilypad isn't Callebaut's only attempt to re-think the design of buildings and cities. Back in 2015, he revealed spectacular plans for the world's first underwater skyscrapers, called Aequorea, which will be 500 meters wide, have 250 floors and be capable of holding 20,000 people. These eco-friendly structures will be self-sufficient, as they'll produce all their own energy, heat, food and water. They'll also be made of 100% recycled plastic, collected from the world's oceans.

Each oceanscraper will have a jellyfish-like structure: the entrance will be located at the surface and then the structure will spiral down to depths of 1000 meters. Inside will be homes, offices and workshops, science laboratories, sea farms and fruit and vegetable gardens. Fresh drinking water will be produced using in-depth pressure to separate salt from seawater.

The Aequorea will be moored off the coast of Brazil, rather than in the open ocean. Residents will certainly be glad of the chance to visit the mainland and soak up some much-needed sunshine at the end of each work week – [6]they'll have been breathing processed air and staring out into the deep, dark ocean all week, after all.

b

Mr. Callebaut's latest project, the Nautilus Eco-Resort in the Philippines, takes its name and inspiration from a mollusk, the nautilus. The hotels themselves will also be shaped like seashells, which will rise and fall as they rotate around a central coil. Visitors can expect uninterrupted sunshine throughout the day as the towers follow the course of the sun. Some rooms will even disappear underground [7]when they're not being used. But before you book your ticket, be warned that [8]the resort isn't about to open any time soon – like most of Mr. Callebaut's designs, it's still some way from actually being built.

The Nautilus Eco-Resort aims to be a 'zero-emission, zero-waste, zero-poverty' project, built entirely from reused or recycled materials from the islands. Visitors will also be actively involved with scientists, engineers and ecologists to ensure their experience encourages sustainable progress. So if you do decide to take a luxury vacation there, [9]you won't be spending all your time lounging around by the pool. You'll also get some practical lessons on sustainability [10]while you're collecting garbage from the beach!

c

Glossary

- **brink (n)** the point in time when something very bad or very good is about to happen
- **irrevocable (adj)** impossible to change or stop
- **moor (v)** to stop a ship or boat from moving by fastening it to a place with ropes or by using an anchor
- **sustainable (adj)** using methods that do not harm the environment
- **visionary (adj)** original and showing a lot of imagination

LISTENING

A SPEAK Work in pairs. Read *(Very) Smart Materials*. Discuss why each material mentioned might be useful.

Glossary

smart materials (n) technologically advanced materials with properties (e.g. color, shape, magnetism, etc) that can change in response to stimuli such as light, temperature, pressure or moisture

(VERY) SMART MATERIALS

1

COLOR-CHANGING PAINT:
The roof and walls of a building automatically change color during the day, depending on the temperature.

3

PIEZOELECTRIC SHOES:
Walking in the shoes causes crystals in the soles to change shape, generating an electric current.

2

SHAPE-CHANGING AIRPLANE WINGS:
The wings detect the plane's height (using atmospheric pressure) and change shape automatically.

4

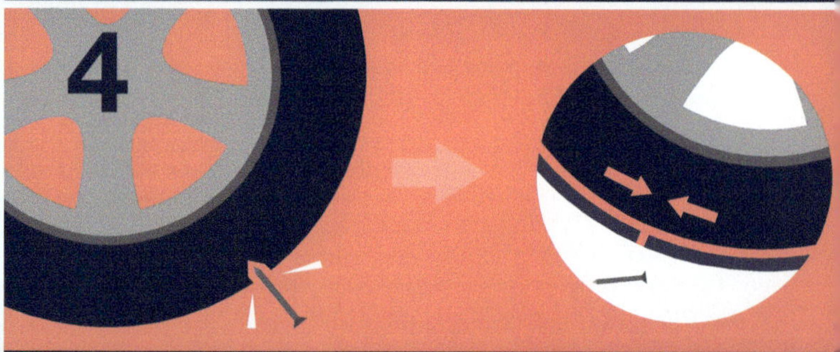

SELF-REPAIRING RUBBER TIRES:
The rubber contains tiny balls of glue. If the tire is damaged, the balls open, glue is released and solidifies, and the holes are repaired.

3.1 **B LISTEN FOR DETAIL** Listen to a conversation about smart materials. Choose the correct options (a, b or c) to answer the questions.

1 What is the woman trying to do?
  a make friendly conversation
  b teach the man something
  c sell something
2 How does the hat work?
  a Its fibers change shape to control air flow.
  b It uses electricity to warm your head.
  c You can adjust its shape based on the weather.
3 What must the man do to keep the hat?
  a write a detailed report about his experiences of wearing it
  b pay $50
  c test it in the rain
4 Why does the woman call her boss?
  a to ask for advice about the jacket
  b to persuade her boss to lower the price
  c to put the man under pressure to buy the jacket

3.1 **C LISTEN FOR TECHNIQUES** Listen again. Which persuasive techniques does the woman use for 1–6? Use the information in the box to help you.

Listening to identify persuasive techniques

People sometimes use tricks to persuade us to do things. When someone is trying to persuade you, listen for these tricks.

Exaggeration: listen for words like *absolutely* and *extremely*.

Leading questions: listen for questions that 'push' you toward a particular answer, including question tags (e.g. *isn't it?*).

Personalization: listen for phrases like *if you imagine* and overuse of *you/your*.

1 biking more frequently ____________
2 how the hat works ____________
3 testing the hat ____________
4 the problem and the solution ____________
5 the smart jacket ____________
6 paying for the jacket ____________

D SPEAK Work in pairs. Discuss the questions.

1 Is it acceptable to use techniques like these to persuade or manipulate other people? In what situations is it OK? When is it unfair?
2 What techniques do you use when you're trying to persuade someone?

PRONUNCIATION
Sounding persuasive

3.2 **A** Listen to the extracts which include the sentences below. How is the woman trying to sound persuasive? Use the information in the box to help you.

1. You just look like a very healthy and athletic person.
2. Yeah, tell me about it!
3. Hmm, I know exactly what you mean.
4. I think you got yourself an excellent deal there, sir. I can see you're a very smart negotiator!
5. You know what? Maybe I can help you out there.
6. But … hmm … maybe … I can offer you … a special price … to thank you for your help.

Sounding persuasive

a Speak fairly quietly (as if you're sharing a secret) and slowly, with a lot of pauses (as if you're thinking of new ideas while speaking).

b Start fast and then slow right down, placing extra stress on all positive words.

c Use slightly exaggerated rising and falling intonation on key words to express emotions.

B SPEAK Work in pairs. Practice saying the sentences in Exercise A as persuasively as possible.

VOCABULARY
Forming verbs from adjectives

A Complete the extracts with the correct form of the verbs in the box.

ensure formalize simplify strengthen tighten warm

1. I bet you can't wait for the weather ________________ up!
2. It's fairly complicated technology, but I'll try ________________ it for you.
3. The fibers in your hat respond to the cold temperature by ________________ up.
4. That ________________ there's no heat loss from your head.
5. As the hat gets wet, the water ________________ the fibers.
6. I just need you to sign this form ________________ our agreement.

B What adjective is each verb from Exercise A formed from?

C Use the affixes in the box to create verbs. The same affix is used for all words in each group. Other spelling changes may also be needed. One group doesn't require any change.

-en -ify en- -ize

1	strong	long	short
2	final	visual	equal
3	empty	smooth	narrow
4	pure	solid	simple
5	danger	able	large

D Complete the advice with the verbs you formed in Exercise C. Sometimes more than one answer is possible.

How to be *persuasive*

1. Don't just offer weak opinions. ________________ your arguments with evidence and examples.
2. Help your potential customers to ________________ themselves using your product.
3. Don't try to persuade everybody at the same time: ________________ your focus to a small group of key people.
4. ________________ complicated explanations to make them easier to understand.
5. ________________ the decision-making process for your customers by removing any barriers that make their decisions harder.
6. Don't speak too quickly. Try to ________________ the pauses between key words.

SPEAKING HUB

A PREPARE Work in pairs. You are going to try to persuade somebody to buy a product made from smart materials. Choose one of the ideas from Listening Exercise A or use your own idea.

B DISCUSS Discuss how your product works and why it's useful.

C PLAN Plan a sales strategy using the persuasion techniques from Listening Exercise C.

D PRESENT Swap partners. Take turns to try to persuade your new partner to buy your product.

E REFLECT Share your experiences with the class. Would you buy your partner's product? Why/Why not?

- Make predictions about the future
- Use persuasive language to sell something

3.2 Better … or worse?

- Discuss progress and society
- Evaluate costs and benefits

P – stress-shift words
V – verb–noun collocations
G – negative inversion
S – reading to determine costs and benefits

LISTENING

A SPEAK Work in groups. Do you think life is generally getting better or worse for your generation?

3.3 **B LISTEN FOR MAIN IDEA** Listen to the first part of a radio show. Match the people (1–5) with the opinions (a–e).

1 Bob ___
2 Mary ___
3 James ___
4 Callum ___
5 Sonia ___

a I'm more aware of bad things happening than I was.
b The earlier generation didn't have the same financial worries as we do.
c Everything was better when I was younger.
d Young people were more polite in the past.
e I feel bad when I compare myself with others.

C SPEAK Work in pairs and discuss the questions.

1 Do you agree with the interviewees' opinions?
2 What are some possible explanations for their opinions?

3.4 **D LISTEN FOR GIST** Listen to the second part of the radio show. Match the opinions (a–e) in Exercise B with the concepts (1–5).

1 the inequality paradox ___
2 the reminiscence bump ___
3 the them-and-us delusion ___
4 the invisible struggle phenomenon ___
5 the window-on-the-world effect ___

3.4 **E LISTEN FOR DETAIL** Listen to the second part again. Are these sentences true (T) or false (F)? Correct the false sentences.

1 Professor Martinelli believes that life is getting better everywhere. T / F
2 Declinism proves that things really are getting worse. T / F
3 When average levels of well-being improve, it can lead to a rise in declinism. T / F
4 People usually have nostalgia for their youth. T / F
5 We tend to focus on good behavior in groups that we don't belong to. T / F
6 Professor Martinelli's parents never worried about financial problems. T / F
7 Professor Martinelli is optimistic that people will try to prevent global tragedies. T / F

F SPEAK Work in pairs. Discuss the questions.

1 What are your experiences of the five concepts from the radio show?
2 Are you generally optimistic or pessimistic about the near future?

PRONUNCIATION
Stress-shift words

3.5 **A Listen to the sentences. Underline the stressed syllables in the words in bold.**

1. Despite amazing **progress** in technology and sharp **increases** in living standards, many of us believe our quality of life has actually **decreased**!
2. Let's hear a few **extracts** from those interviews.
3. You feel like a **reject** from society.
4. It's almost as if we **rewrite** the events in our memories.
5. You've simply erased their negative **attributes** and bad **conduct** from your memory.
6. We tend to **attribute** other people's success to luck.
7. That's a major source of inter-generational **conflict**: young adults always **suspect** that earlier generations had it much easier!

3.6 **B Underline the stressed syllables in the words in bold. Then listen and check.**

1. Why are you always such a **rebel**? Why do you always **rebel** against everything I say?
2. I didn't think I'd like Thai food, but now I'm a **convert**. Your cooking has **converted** me!
3. You need to install an **upgrade** for your computer. When did you last **upgrade** it?
4. I deal with **imports** and **exports** in my job: I **import** raw materials and **export** finished products to customers.
5. I **frequent** this café during the summer, but I'm not really a **frequent** visitor during the rest of the year.

C Practice saying the sentences with the correct stress.

GRAMMAR
Negative inversion

A Complete the extracts from the radio show with one word.

1. No sooner ________ **an older person gotten on the bus** than we all stood up.
2. Only after they'd all gotten off the bus ________ **I finally sit down**.
3. No way **could I** ________ **afford an apartment**.
4. None of our neighbors had much money, and neither ________ **we**.
5. Not ________ **did I have great friends**, but we also did cool things all the time.
6. By no means ________ **I suggesting** that life is wonderful for everybody everywhere.
7. ________ in a million years **did it occur to me** that my parents were worried about money.

B WORK IT OUT Match the sentences (1–7) in Exercise A with the rules (a–d) in the box.

> **Negative inversion**
>
> When we want to emphasize a negative element of a sentence (e.g. *never*), we can move it to the beginning and swap the subject and auxiliary verb. This process is called inversion.
>
> a When there is no auxiliary verb, we add *do/does/did.* ___ ___ ___
>
> b Inversion with *could* is common after phrases like *only after* and *no way*. ___ ___
>
> c Inversion is very common in the structure *not only … but also*. ___
>
> d After *no sooner*, we need a *than*-clause. ___
>
> We don't use inversion when a negative word/phrase is the subject: *Not one person offered me a seat.* (NOT: ~~did offer~~)

C Go to the Grammar Hub on page X.

D Complete the sentences so they are true for you.

1. Under no circumstances would I …
2. Only rarely do I …
3. Not only do I think …

SPEAKING

A PREPARE Work in pairs. Imagine you are on a radio interview about progress. Student A – read the information below. Student B – go to the Communication Hub on page XXIII.

B SPEAK Role-play your interview.

Student A

> You're a radio interviewer. You believe that while people complain about the world today, overall it is actually getting better. Interview Student B about progress. Also give your view on the subject.
>
> Discuss the following areas.
>
> - the impact of technology
> - community
> - quality of life
> - cost of living
> - employment
> - the environment

READING

A PREDICT Work in pairs. Discuss the questions.

1 Look at the pictures and title of the article. What do you think 'voluntourism' might be?

2 What do you think attracts people to these kinds of activities?

3 Why might some voluntary work do more harm than good?

B SKIM Read *Voluntourism: more harm than good?* quickly and check your ideas in Exercise A.

C READ FOR COSTS AND BENEFITS Work in pairs. What are the deep costs and benefits of voluntourism? Use the information in the box to help you.

Reading to determine costs and benefits

When you read a for-and-against, or pro and con, article, it's useful to distinguish between **surface-level** costs/benefits (e.g. obvious, short-term or unimportant ones) and **deep** costs/benefits (e.g. hidden, long-term or highly important ones). When deciding whether you agree with the writer's opinion, focus mainly on the deep costs and benefits.

VOLUNTOURISM

more harm than good?

When Pippa Biddle was a teenager, she went on a school trip to Tanzania, where she and her classmates were tasked with building a library for an orphanage. Lacking even basic construction skills, they did their best and, remarkably, over the course of a week, the building started to take shape. Only later did Pippa learn the truth: every night, a group of professional builders had been carefully undoing and redoing the teenagers' work in order to make the construction structurally sound. The whole project was an illusion: the true purpose wasn't to get help on the building project, but to make the teenagers feel good about themselves.

Welcome to the world of voluntourism, where volunteering meets tourism. Unlike true volunteering, this is paid work – but it's the worker who pays for the privilege. On the surface, voluntourism is a win–win situation. The voluntourist seizes an opportunity to travel to an exotic country and work with real people in authentic locations, while the recipients get free help. But the reality, as Pippa's story brings home to us, is somewhat more complicated.

The main criticism of voluntourism is that it perpetuates the myth that people in some countries need help from wise and generous benefactors in richer countries. The reality, of course, is that these countries have plenty of kind-hearted experts of their own. But of course, most voluntourists aren't even experts: they're typically students looking for a quick adventure, with no valuable skills to offer. At best, their input is frequently a waste of time. At worst, it could do more harm than good, as with Pippa's building experience.

Even worse are stories of fake projects created merely to keep the volunteers busy, regardless of any inherent local need. For example, there are English-language schools in remote communities where the locals neither want nor need to study English.

It's hard to avoid the conclusion that voluntourism is nothing more than an ego-trip: a chance to pretend you're making the world a better place, so you can wow your friends back home with tales of your generosity, your suffering and your profound experience of 'finding yourself'.

But there's another side to volunteerism. While many people do sign up with naïve expectations, they frequently emerge from their experiences with a far deeper understanding. On their return home, they can spread a more positive and realistic image of the countries they visit, and counter rather than perpetuate stereotypes. Finally, many voluntourists go on to become committed life-long volunteers, with their new-found habit of helping others, whether globally or in their own communities.

It's also an oversimplification to claim that voluntourism is always harmful to local communities. Highly-skilled volunteers like doctors, scientists and engineers can indeed bring real benefits. The key is to do so in a spirit of cooperation and mutual respect with local experts, rather than following the 'watch me and learn' approach. Many voluntourism agencies can have a genuinely positive impact both on the volunteers and the communities they serve.

So if you're considering signing up as a voluntourist, seize the initiative and do some research beforehand. Be honest and realistic about your skills and expectations. Above all, never forget that the main beneficiary of your voluntourism adventure will probably be you. With the right mindset, this could well be the most important experience of your life.

D READ FOR DETAIL Work in pairs. Read the article again and discuss the questions.

1. Why did the builders work at night?
2. How did Pippa's building experience 'do more harm than good'?
3. What does the writer mean by 'the right mindset' in the last paragraph?

E SPEAK Work in groups. Do you think voluntourism does more harm than good? Would you consider doing it yourself?

VOCABULARY

Verb–noun collocations

A Choose a verb to complete each pair of verb–noun collocations. Then decide on the best collocation to complete each sentence. Use the information in the box to help you.

> **Verb–noun collocations**
>
> Verb–noun collocations are a good way to build vocabulary. Sometimes these include advanced verbs (e.g. *perpetuate*), but mostly they include very common verbs (e.g. *make, do, take*). Try to underline these as you read in English.

1. Unless you have valuable work experience you'll usually ________ *your best* / *more harm than good*.
2. Volunteer organizations should always ________ the *time* / *shape* to train volunteers before a project.
3. A trained English teacher can ________ *benefits* / *home* to a host community.
4. It's vital that voluntourists ________ *the responsibility* / *the opportunity* to understand their host community before and during their visit.
5. Volunteer organizations should not ________ the *myth* / *problem* that their projects are just extended vacations.

B Go to the Vocabulary Hub on page XVII.

C SPEAK Work in pairs. Do you agree with sentences 1–5 in Exercise A? Why/Why not?

SPEAKING HUB

A PREPARE Work in pairs. Imagine you are going to volunteer in another country. Choose one of the following voluntary projects or use your own idea.

- working at an animal sanctuary
- planting trees
- teaching children
- cleaning up trash

B PLAN Create a list of surface-level and deep costs and benefits for:

- you and your partner
- who you are helping
- the world in general.

C DISCUSS Discuss whether the benefits outweigh the costs. How could the costs be reduced? How could the benefits be increased?

D PRESENT Present your plans to the class. Whose ideas would have the best chance of making the world a better place?

Glossary

beneficiary (n) someone who gets an advantage from a situation
illusion (n) a false or wrong belief or idea
mindset (n) a way of thinking about things
orphan (n) a child whose parents have died
perpetuate (v) to make something such as a situation or process continue, especially one that is wrong, unfair or dangerous
profound (adj) used about very strong feelings
recipient (n) someone who receives something

- Discuss progress and society
- Evaluate costs and benefits

Café Hub

3.3 Sustainability

Ⓐ the 'rule of three' Ⓢ maintaining a conversation

Seaweed farming

A Work in small groups. What is being shown in each picture (a–e)?

B Watch the video. Check your ideas to Exercise A and number pictures a–e in the order they appear.

a ☐

b ☐

c ☐

d ☐

e ☐

C Watch the video again. Answer the questions.

1. What have scientists discovered about seaweed?
2. What can seaweed help us do?
3. What are the three countries mentioned in the video?
4. Is the presenter's tone generally positive, negative or neutral?

Glossary

allotment (n) a small piece of land in town you can rent and use for growing vegetables
harvest (v) to pick and collect crops or plants
seaweed (n) a green or brown plant that grows in the sea

AUTHENTIC ENGLISH

A Work in pairs. Read the sentence from the video and the information in the box. What three things doesn't seaweed need?

This doesn't need lots of land space to grow it, it doesn't need awful artificial fertilizers, it doesn't need lots of fresh water.

The 'rule of three'

The 'rule of three' is a rhetorical device we use to express concepts more completely, emphasize our points and increase the memorability of our message. In the 'rule of three', we frequently repeat the same grammatical construction.

B Work in pairs. Complete the sentences using your own ideas and the 'rule of three'.

1. To succeed in life, you need to work hard, you need *to have passion* and you need *to have a role model*.
2. I'm ready to start the day. My face is washed, my ______ and my ______.
3. Maria was the ideal employee – she was always on time, she always ______ and she ______.
4. The current government has ruined the economy, it ______ and it ______.
5. I told the sales clerk I wanted to exchange the item, ______ or ______.
6. I ______. You ______. The whole class ______.

C Compare your sentences with another pair.

D Work in small groups. Write sentences with the 'rule of three' to say what you need to do to learn a language successfully.

Fueling the future

SAM MALCOLM AMANDA HARRY EMILY

A Work in pairs. Discuss the questions.

1 Do you prefer to use public transportation or travel by car? Why?

2 What do you think about policies that ban or limit cars in city centers?

B Watch the video. Are these statements true (T) or false (F)? Correct the false sentences.

1 Malcolm has recently achieved a long-held ambition. T / F

2 Amanda understands the appeal of owning a sports car. T / F

3 Malcolm believes speed is the main positive of car ownership. T / F

4 Amanda says that all new vehicles will be banned from the UK by 2040. T / F

5 Amanda thinks that other feasible options besides gas vehicles currently exist. T / F

6 Harry thinks alternative fuels will be the norm in the distant future. T / F

7 Malcolm is going to let Amanda test drive his car. T / F

SPEAKING SKILL

A Watch the video again. Complete the sentences (1–6) from the video.

1 ______________________ coming out for a look at my new wheels?

2 I mean we don't really need them in the city. ______________________?

3 ______________________ Harry? You're a cool young guy ... you must like sports cars.

4 Just the other day we were discussing alternative fuels, ______________________?

5 That kind of thing, must be a long way off though, ______________________?

6 ______________________ Malcolm?

B Work in pairs. Look at your answers in Exercise A. What are the speakers doing in each sentence?

1 Malcolm is asking Amanda to give her opinion.

Maintaining a conversation

Inviting people to give their opinion or speak

Ask a direct question (*Would you like to say something here, Andy?*) or invite someone to speak using a statement (*You haven't said anything yet, Maria.*)

Noticing changes in attitude

Respond to body language and facial expressions by asking questions or making statements. (*I can tell you don't agree with me.*)

Question tags

Add these to a statement to make it a question or to request agreement. (*I think we all pretty much agree on this, don't we?*)

Asking questions to get agreement

Ask people directly to agree with you in order to move conversations along. (*Am I right in thinking that's true?*)

C Work in pairs. Choose one of the topics below and try to maintain a conversation for four minutes without any long pauses.

- the environment
- a documentary you watched recently
- public transportation in your country

SPEAKING HUB

A PREPARE Work in a small group. Think about the pros and cons of the sources of energy below.

- wind power
- tidal power
- fossil fuels
- nuclear power
- solar power

B PLAN You are going to discuss which of the energies would be the best for achieving a sustainable future with another group. Plan how you are going to achieve agreement within your group and get all the members of the group to give their opinion.

A: What's your opinion?

B: Tidal power is too expensive compared to other renewable sources.

C DISCUSS Join with another group to discuss the pros and cons of the sources of energy.

D REFLECT As a class decide which arguments were the most convincing and which of the energy sources are necessary for a sustainable future.

Discuss renewable energy

➤ Turn to page XXVI to learn how to write a persuasive email about sustainability.

Unit 3 Review

VOCABULARY

A **Complete the brochure with the words in the box. There are two extra words that you do not need to use.**

accumulate	biodegradable	consume	depletion
emissions	exploitation	neutral	offset	renewable

Want to live a more

sustainable life?

Here's how.

1 Stop buying products wrapped in plastic, which _______________ in the oceans. Choose products that use _______________ packaging instead.

2 Cut down on the energy you _______________, and use solar power, wind power or other _______________ energy sources if possible.

3 Reduce your _______________ of greenhouse gases by walking or biking instead of driving.

4 Become carbon-_______________ by planting trees to _______________ the carbon you generate.

B **Complete the sentences with the correct form of the word in parentheses.**

1. They want to _______________ (*large*) our college by adding a new building.
2. The dirty water is _______________ (*pure*) before being released into the sea.
3. If your dinner's cold, you can _______________ (*warm*) it up in the microwave.
4. They're _______________ (*strong*) the old bridge before it falls down.
5. We didn't bother to _______________ (*formal*) our agreement – we trust each other.
6. Some screws are loose on this table. Can you _______________ (*tight*) them up?
7. We were winning six-five, but the other team _______________ (*equal*) in the last minute.

C **Complete the conversation with one verb in each space.**

A: I want to [1] _______________ the world a better place, but I don't know how. Could you [2] _______________ me in the right direction?

B: The only thing that [3] _______________ to mind is voluntourism.

A: Good idea! I'll go for it.

B: Well, please don't [4] _______________ this personally, but you don't really have any skills to offer. They have strict rules about who they accept.

A: Really? Maybe they'll [5] _______________ an exception for me.

B: No, I think you need to [6] _______________ the time to research it carefully so you don't end up [7] _______________ more harm than good.

A: OK, thanks for the advice. I'll try to [8] _______________ it on board.

GRAMMAR

A **Find and correct the mistakes in four of the sentences.**

1. Fifty years from now, the world will have been changing completely.
2. My life's about getting a lot more complicated.
3. We'll be seeing a lot more of each other when we're neighbors.
4. Call me again at ten – I might have finished by then.
5. I'm on the verge of resigning from my job.
6. Your eyes will hurt after you'll have been studying all night.
7. Prices setting to fall by 10% over the next year.

B **Reorder the words to make sentences. The first word is given in bold.**

1. **By** / you / do / I / should / means / believe / no / resign
   _______________________________________.
2. **Under** / be / opened / may / circumstances / no / this box
   _______________________________________.
3. **Not** / did / thanked / all the work / you / have / me / once / for / I
   _______________________________________.
4. **Only** / the waiter / our food / three times / we / bring / complained / had / after / did
   _______________________________________.
5. **No** / the laundry / started / had / than / put out / sooner / it / I / to rain
   _______________________________________.
6. **No** / to college / ever / going back / I / way / consider / would
   _______________________________________.
7. **Not** / this hard / since / worked / students / we / have / I / were
   _______________________________________.

4 INTELLIGENCE

> I know that I am intelligent because I know that I know nothing.
>
> Socrates

Future choices at the Istituto Italiano Di Tecnologia, Genoa.

OBJECTIVES

- discuss improving the brain
- talk about future technology
- talk about regrets
- discuss intelligence
- recount events
- write a report

Work with a partner. Discuss the questions.

1 Look at the picture. How is it connected to the topic of intelligence?

2 Read the quote. What do you think Socrates means? Do you agree?

3 Would you rather be very intelligent, very strong or very attractive? Why?

4.1 Brain training

- Discuss improving the brain
- Talk about future technology

G conditionals without *if* V conceptual metaphors P adding information S identifying logical fallacies

LISTENING

A Work in pairs. Look at the brain teaser below. Do you know the answer? Go to the **Communication Hub** on **page XX** for more brain teasers.

TODAY'S BRAIN TEASER

David's mother had three children.
The first one was named April.
The second one was named May.
What was the name of the third child?

4.1 **B LISTEN FOR GIST** Listen to a radio discussion about ways to increase your brain power. What four methods of boosting brain power are discussed?

1 ______
2 ______
3 ______
4 ______

4.2 **C LISTEN AND IDENTIFY** Listen to three extracts from the radio discussion. Whose argument is weaker in each extract? Which type of logical fallacy (a–c) from the box have they used?

Identifying logical fallacies

a **Generalization:** drawing a conclusion about a large group from a very small amount of data.
b **Anecdotal evidence:** using non-scientific personal experience as proof for something.
c **False cause:** claiming a relationship exists between two things when there is no evidence to support this.

1 *Dr. Carter / Amanda* ___
2 *Dr. Carter / Amanda* ___
3 *Dr. Carter / Amanda* ___

D SPEAK Work in pairs and discuss the questions.

1 Which of the methods that the speakers discussed do you think can really boost people's brainpower?
2 Do you agree with what Dr. Carter said about Sudoku?
3 Why do you think findings have been inconclusive on some methods?

PRONUNCIATION

Adding information

A Underline the part(s) of these sentences that provide additional information about something.

1 To answer the question, I'm joined today by two experts, Dr. Ramona Carter, a leading neuroscientist, and Amanda Saraha, a life coach and the author of *How to be smarter*.
2 So for example, if you do a lot of Sudoku, the math puzzle where you write the numbers in boxes, it's most likely that you will just become better at playing that game.
3 Recently, we've seen a lot of media stories about super foods, food that you should eat to boost your brain power.

4.3 **B** Listen to the sentences in Exercise A. Draw arrows where the intonation rises or falls.

C SPEAK Work in pairs. Give additional information about the underlined words.

1 I like to do some exercise before I start work in the mornings. (give more detail)
2 My friend is definitely one of the smartest people I know. (give more detail)
3 I try to do some meditation because it helps me relax. (define the word)

VOCABULARY

Conceptual metaphors

A **Match the sentences (1–6) with the related conceptual metaphor (a–c). Use the information in the box to help you.**

> **Conceptual metaphors**
>
> Conceptual metaphors help us to talk about abstract or complex ideas by comparing them with something else. For example, life is frequently compared with a journey, such as in sentences like this:
>
> *She had reached a crossroads. Should she go to college or continue with her job?* (= reached a point when she needed to make an important decision about her life)

1 I spent an hour doing Sudoku. ___
2 She shot down my arguments. ___
3 He has a really fiery temper. ___
4 After I had cooled down, I apologized. ___
5 I've invested a lot of time in brain training. ___
6 I couldn't defend my position. ___

a anger = heat
b argument = war
c time = money

B **Read three sentences from the radio show. What do the underlined words and phrases mean?**

1 Of course, everyone would like to be more intelligent, but is it really possible? And if so, how can we make ourselves brighter?
2 A team from Cambridge actually tried to shed some light on the impact of brain training games.
3 As Dr. Carter says, we may still be in the dark about the science behind it, but I personally believe that the food we eat has a huge effect on every aspect of our lives.

C **SPEAK** **Identify the conceptual metaphor being used in the questions. Then discuss the questions in pairs.**

1 Do you think brain training is a waste of time?
2 What's a good strategy to convince people to buy brain-training products?
3 Do you think intelligent people are usually more hot-tempered?
4 Are you able to stay cool in an argument?

SPEAKING

A Look at the advertisements. Which products would you try? Which would you avoid? Why?

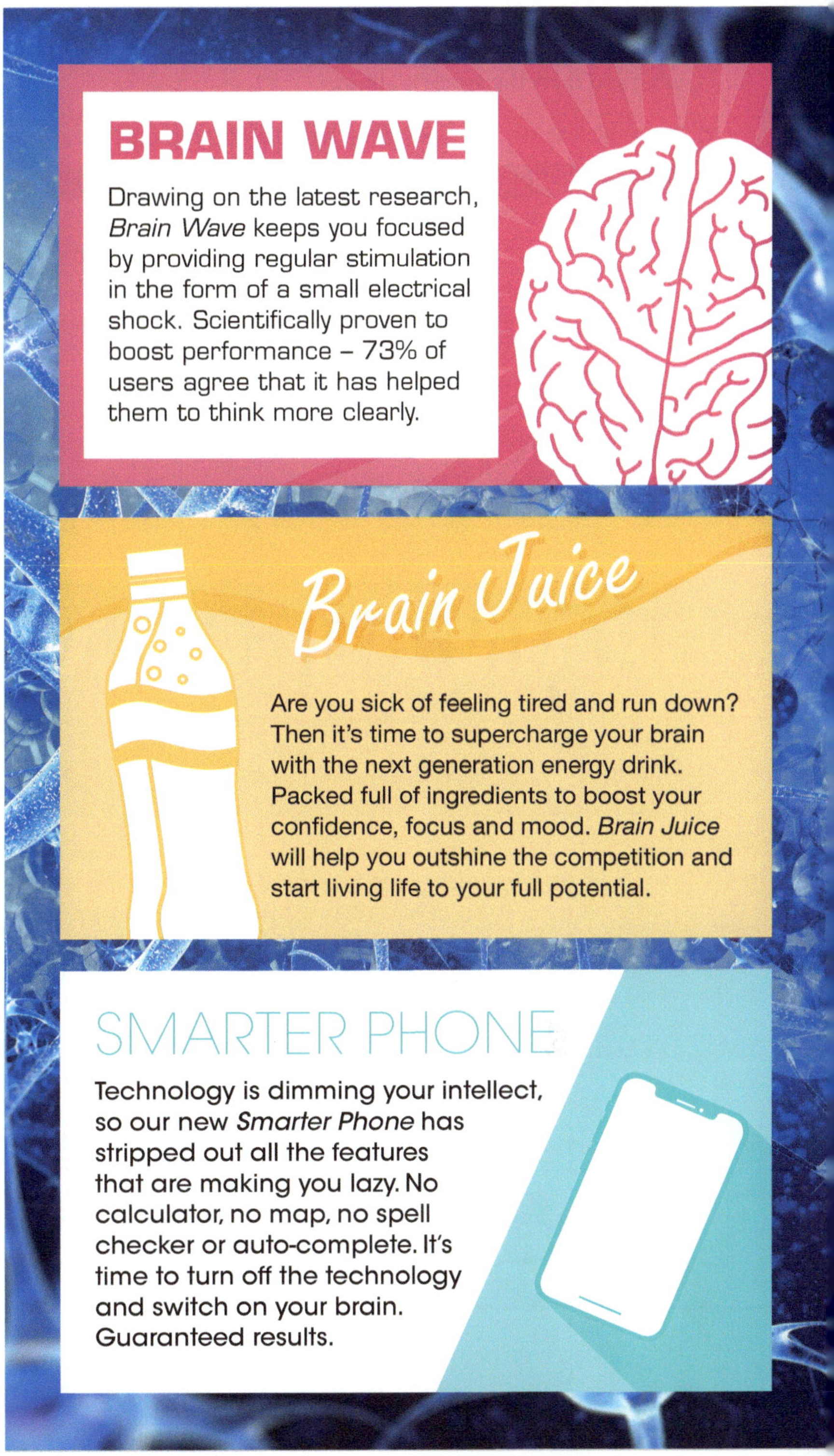

B **PRESENT** Work in groups. Think of a product or service that you could sell to people who wanted to boost their brain power. Present the product to the class. Which product is the most popular?

C **DISCUSS** Work in pairs and discuss the questions.

1 Do you believe that it's really possible to make yourself smarter?
2 Should companies be allowed to sell products like the ones in Exercise A? Why/Why not?

READING

A SPEAK Work in pairs. If you could significantly boost your intelligence overnight, would you do it? Why/Why not?

B PREDICT Work in pairs. Look at *Brain augmentation: The key to super intelligence*. In your own words, explain to your partner what you think the article is about.

C READ FOR MAIN IDEA Read the article and complete the table.

	Method of augmentation	Examples of benefits
1		
2		
3		

D READ FOR DETAIL Read the article again and answer the questions.

1 When do scientists predict highly sophisticated robots will be a common sight?

2 How has technology been used to help blind people?

3 What did scientists learn from the research with epilepsy patients?

4 What potential dangers of brain augmentation does the article mention?

E SPEAK Work in pairs and discuss the questions.

1 What was the most surprising thing that you learned from the article?

2 Do you think that the government should control this kind of augmentation?

BRAIN AUGMENTATION:

The key to super intelligence

How far would you go to enhance your own intelligence? Would you implant a chip into your brain? For many scientists around the world, the answer appears to be *yes*. Brain augmentation, enhancing the intelligence of human brains with implants, is a growing area of interest as some predict that super-intelligent cyborgs will be a normal part of everyday life within the next 10 to 20 years.

In fact, experts believe that there are three main approaches to brain augmentation: interfacing with the brain, stimulating the brain and enhancing the brain with implants.

Suppose that a computer could interface with a brain, it could record information, store it, and even use this information for some other purpose – such as sharing it with others. In theory, if people's brains were linked through the internet, they could benefit from each others' knowledge.

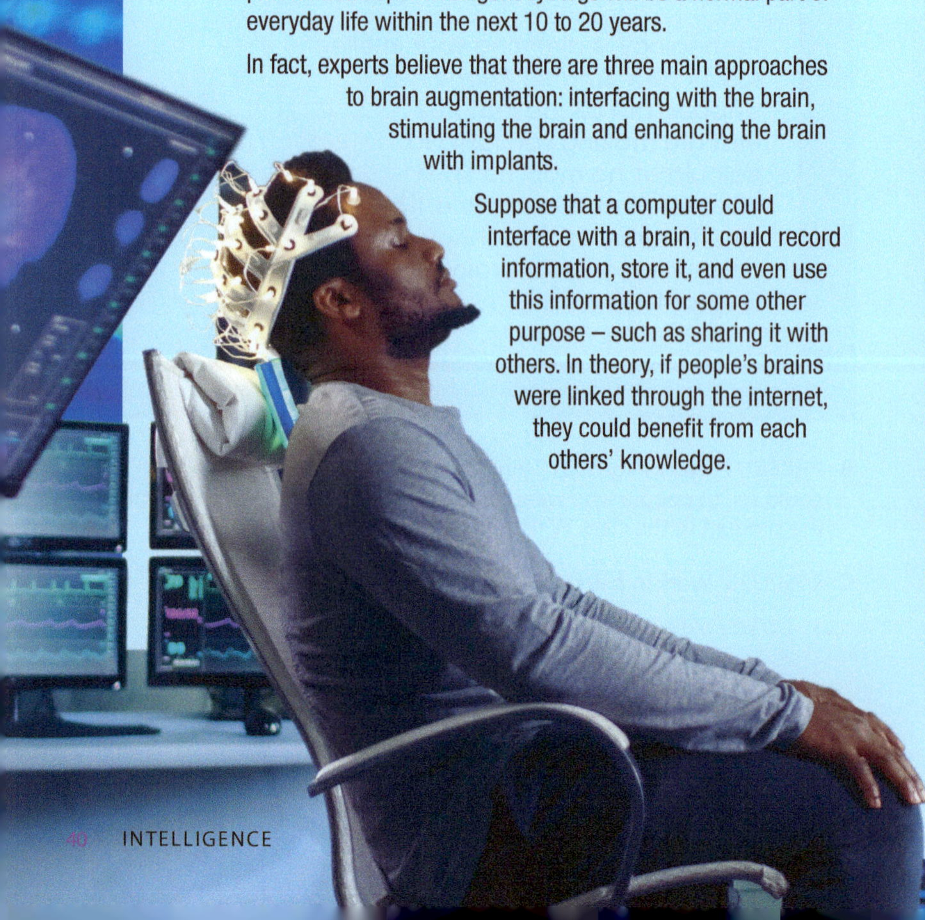

Another way of augmenting the brain is by stimulating it in some way – typically with electricity. One goal of stimulation is to produce artificial sensations, such as the sensation of touch or vision. In this case, the main motivation comes from a desire to help repair the brains of people with neurological conditions. For example, in the last couple of years, scientists from *Second Sight* have been able to partially restore the sight of some blind people by implanting a chip into their retinas that sends signals to the brain from a camera. Although these people cannot see, the stimulation of the brain creates pictures in their mind. Right now these are just black and white, pixelated images, but assuming that the technology continues to improve, this could be the beginning of a permanent cure for blindness.

Another goal of stimulating the brain is to improve its function and its capabilities. A recent study led by Dong Song of the University of Southern California looked at the effects of stimulating the brain on memory. Researchers worked with twenty volunteers who were having electrodes implanted into their brains to treat epilepsy. Researchers examined the effects of stimulating the brain through these electrodes during tests that involved either the volunteers' short-term memory or working memory and found that the right kind of stimulation improved short-term memory by 15% and working memory by 25%. Interestingly, unless the right kind of stimulation was provided, the volunteers' memory was actually worse. So, there is clearly a lot of work to be done to understand the right kind of stimulation to provide.

GRAMMAR

Conditionals without *if*

A **Underline conditional sentences in the article with the same meaning as sentences (1–6).**

1. If a computer could connect to a brain, it could download information and make it available to others. (Paragraph 3)
2. If the technology gets better, it could lead to a cure for blindness. (Paragraph 4)
3. If robots decided to fight against humans, we would have to be smart enough to take them on. (Paragraph 6)
4. If people created successful brain-augmentation implants, we would need to think about the moral implications. (Paragraph 7)
5. If you ask many people about what's happening right now, they will tell you they don't know anything about it. (Paragraph 8)
6. If the government had not allowed this work into augmentation, we would not be developing innovations to assist people with vision problems. (Paragraph 8)

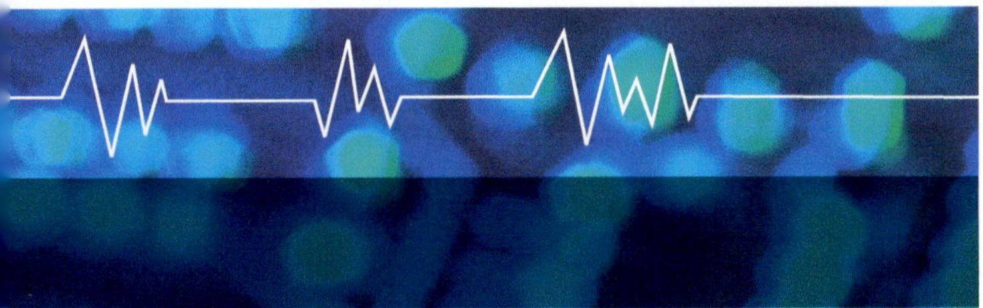

The final approach to augmentation is the most radical, because it involves merging man and machine. The biggest impact is likely to be from implanting a chip into your brain. Bryan Johnson, founder and CEO of neuroscience company Kernel, believes that these chips could be used to help us learn faster, enhance our memories, and provide us with a cognitive boost. *Space X* and *Tesla* are also working on technology to boost the human brain through the company Neuralink. One concern raised is that humans are able to enhance their intelligence, because, should AI turn against humans in the future, we would need to be smart enough to fight back.

Of course, were brain-boosting implants to be successfully developed, they would raise several difficult ethical questions. Would changing people's brains change their personalities? If someone had an implant fitted, would they be at risk of being hacked? Could these super intelligent cyborgs be a danger to the rest of us?

Ask many people about what's happening right now in this field and they will tell you they are completely in the dark. Unfortunately that includes the government, who many feel should be doing more to regulate the technology and ensure that it really is safe. However, had the government banned this kind of research, the technology to help blind people would not be under development.

B **Choose the correct words to complete the rules (a–c). Then look at the example sentences you found in Exercise A to complete the rules (d–f).**

Conditionals without *if*

We can use inversions to talk about hypothetical situations in formal or literary English:

- **a** *Had*: We use *had* + subject + ***infinitive*** / ***past participle*** / ***base form***.
- **b** *Should*: We use *should* + subject + ***infinitive*** / ***past participle*** / ***base form***.
- **c** *Were*: We use *were* + subject + ***infinitive*** / ***past participle*** / ***base form***.

We can use other words instead of *if*:

- **d** Verbs: *imagine*, ________________
- **e** Present participles: ________________, *presuming, providing, supposing*
  - Past participles: *provided*
- **f** We can also make a conditional sentence by starting with an imperative and joining the clauses with ________________.

C Go to the **Grammar Hub** on **page XII**.

D **Change the start of these sentences to make conditionals without *if*. Complete the sentences with your own opinions.**

1. If people were able to upload information into their brains, …
2. If we ignore the potential danger of AI, …
3. If brain implants were only affordable for the super-rich, …
4. If I were to be offered a brain-boosting implant, …

E **Compare your sentences with your partner. Do you agree with your partner's opinions?**

SPEAKING HUB

Work in pairs. Student A – go to the **Communication Hub** on **page XXI**. Student B – go to the **Communication Hub** on **page XXIII**. Describe the situations to your partner. Discuss what you would do.

Glossary

cyborg (n) a creature in science fiction stories that is part human and part machine

electrode (n) a small metal or carbon object inside an electrical cell or a battery that electricity flows through. There are two electrodes, one positive and one negative.

neurological (adj) relating to your nervous system or to the diseases that affect it

retina (n) the part at the back of your eye that sends light signals to your brain, where they are changed into images

Discuss improving the brain

Talk about future technology

4.2 Thinking and thought

- Talk about regrets
- Discuss intelligence

G – wishes and regrets
P – adding information or changing the topic
V – science and research; thinking
S – identifying different writing styles

READING

A SPEAK Read *No need to be embarrassed?* Discuss the following questions.

1 Have any of the situations described happened to you?

2 Which stories do you think are the most and least embarrassing?

B Read *The positive side of embarrassment*. What do scientists think is the purpose of embarrassment?

C READ TO IDENTIFY Who is each text written for? What is the purpose of each text?

Text 1 ______________________________

Text 2 ______________________________

D Read both texts again. Find examples of the writing styles (a–e) in the box. Use the information in the box to help you.

Identifying different writing styles

Texts written for a general audience usually use:

a shorter, simpler sentences (including sentences that start with *and*, *but* and *so*)

b idiomatic language (contractions, phrasal verbs, idioms).

Academic papers and articles:

c are objective not personal (no *I*, *you* or *we*, no emotional adjectives)

d use longer, more complex sentences

e use formal language (no contractions or phrasal verbs, but academic vocabulary).

E SPEAK Work in pairs. Do you agree that displaying embarrassment can make a positive impression on others?

NO NEED TO BE EMBARRASSED?

Glossary

buddy (n) (American English) friend

consolation (n) something that makes you feel less unhappy or disappointed

cringeworthy (adj) something that makes you feel embarrassed or ashamed

Psychologists believe that embarrassment should actually be viewed as a positive thing. When we blush or stammer in embarrassment, we are showing that we know that we shouldn't have said or done something and that we don't normally do this kind of thing. In other words, showing we are embarrassed is a kind of non-verbal apology.

Well that's all well and good, but when you're caught red-faced, I don't think that would be any consolation. In light of this research, I thought I'd do some of my own. Now I'm no stranger to embarrassment, but a quick survey revealed embarrassing work stories far worse than mine. Here are some of your most cringeworthy moments.

"Can you even begin to imagine what it's like to walk into a glass door at full speed? Must be painful, right? Now add to that the mortification that it was in front of your new boss. If I hadn't been trying to impress her with my walking-while-emailing skills – like I was a hot-shot political aide on a TV show – I might have noticed the door. But the humiliation doesn't stop there. All of my co-workers were sitting around a conference table on the other side of that glass door. I would have loved to make a good impression. But all I ended up with was wounded pride … and a broken nose."

"Generally speaking I'm a pretty confident person. I'm great at putting people at ease and keeping conversation going. I just wish I wasn't so absent-minded. Over the years it has caused me infinite amounts of awkwardness. But never more so than just last month. An important client was flying in from Vancouver for an even more important meeting. So I offered to pick him up from the airport. The only problem was by the time he came through the arrivals gate, I had completely forgotten where I'd parked my car. We spent the next two hours wandering aimlessly around various parking lots in the pouring rain. I wish I'd never offered to give him a ride … and I bet he does, too!"

"This happened five years ago but to this very day the memory still haunts me! The CEO where I used to work sent a (very smug) company-wide email congratulating *himself* on record profit margins. In response I wrote a very rude message making fun of the CEO to my office buddy … or so I thought. If only I hadn't been in such a rush to have lunch, I might have noticed that I had hit *reply to all* instead of *reply* … those two little words make a huge difference. My email was sent to every employee in London and Boston. It was only when I came back from lunch and everyone was snickering that it clicked what had happened. I just wanted the ground to swallow me up."

The positive side of embarrassment

The outward signs of embarrassment are well known, and include blushing, gazing downward, turning away and face touching. However, researchers have been attempting to identify the evolutionary purpose of embarrassment.

Several researchers have postulated that embarrassment may help to signal whether humans are willing to develop long-term bonds with each other. For example, Lewis (2008) believes that embarrassment is when individuals make a negative evaluation of their actions, thoughts or feelings because they feel they have not behaved according to social standards.

Feinberg, Willer, Keltner and Dacher (2012) **hypothesised** that embarrassment served several important social functions and **conducted** several **experiments** to test this hypothesis.

In one experiment, **participants** were asked to tell an embarrassing story and then complete a questionnaire that looked at their tendency to be kind. The **findings** indicated that people who showed more embarrassment were more likely to be kinder people. The researchers **concluded** that these people were more 'pro-social' – that is they wanted to be part of the group and not behave in a way that was counter to the social **norms** of the group.

In another experiment, participants witnessed an interaction between a researcher and someone that they thought was another participant (but was actually an actor). The researcher praised the fake participant's performance on a test, and the fake participant either expressed embarrassment or pride. The participants who saw the actor look embarrassed were more likely to think he was trustworthy and want to interact with him. This experiment **demonstrated** that people are more likely to have a positive perception of someone who shows embarrassment. The researchers **speculated** that this was because this person is showing a desire to fit in with the group.

From examining the findings of studies such as these, it appears that the evolutionary purpose of embarrassment was to help identify individuals who would be likely to cooperate with the group. So although embarrassment is widely thought of as a negative emotion, displaying embarrassment most likely makes a positive impression on others.

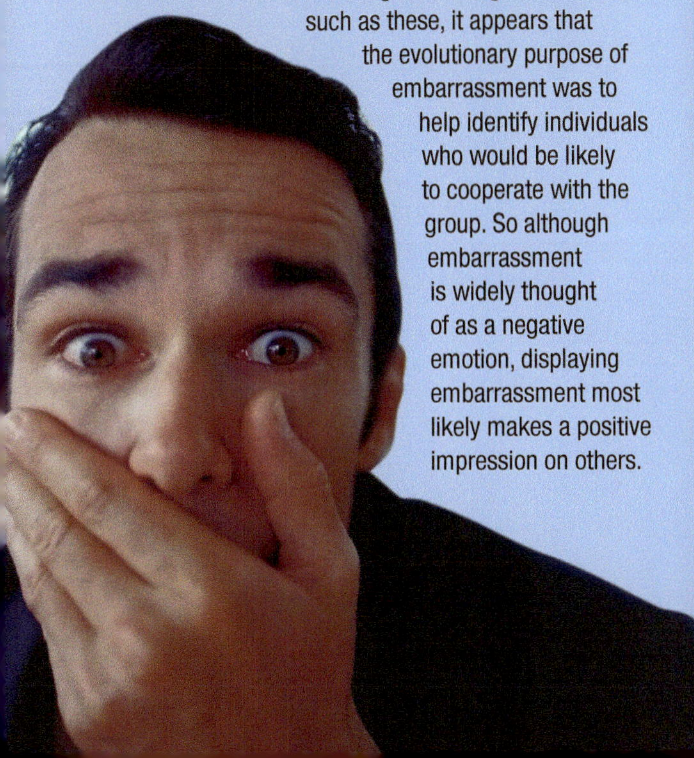

VOCABULARY
Science and research

A Match the words in bold from the second text with the meanings (1–9).

1 do (an experiment, a study) ________
2 standard behavior ________
3 suggest a theory ________
4 guess ________
5 people taking part in a study or experiment ________
6 results ________
7 test ________
8 decide ________
9 show ________

B Go to the **Vocabulary Hub** on **page XVIII**.

C SPEAK Work in pairs and discuss the questions.

1 Would you like to be a participant in a psychology study?
2 Think of an experiment you've heard about. What did it hypothesize? What were the findings?
3 Is it ethical to conduct a study where you make people feel embarrassed?

GRAMMAR
Wishes and regrets

A WORK IT OUT Look at the underlined sentences in *No need to be embarrassed?* Then choose the correct words to complete the rules.

Wishes and regrets

1 We use *wish* or *if only* + simple ***present / past*** to wish that the present was different.
2 We use *wish* or *if only* + ***present / past*** perfect to wish that the past was different.
3 We can use *should (not)* or *ought (not) to* + *have* + *past participle* or *been* + ***present / past*** participle to talk about regrets.
4 We can use *would* + *love* or *prefer* or *hate* + ***to have / have*** + *(not)* past participle to talk about regrets.

B Go to the **Grammar Hub** on **page XII**.

C Complete the sentences so they are true for you.

1 If only I could …
2 I wish I were …
3 I would have loved to …

SPEAKING

A PREPARE Think of a time when you did something you regret. You can use the list of ideas on **page XXI** of the **Communication Hub** or your own ideas. What happened? What do you wish had happened differently?

B DISCUSS Tell your partner about what happened. Listen to your partner and ask questions.

LISTENING

A SPEAK Work in pairs. Look at the pictures. Discuss which of the following gives people the biggest advantage in life. Give reasons for your choice.

- Money
- Intelligence
- Supportive family
- Good health

B LISTEN FOR MAIN IDEA 4.4 You are going to listen to part of a debate about whether being highly intelligent gives people an advantage in life. What are the speaker's three main points?

1 ______________________
2 ______________________
3 ______________________

C LISTEN FOR SPECIFIC INFORMATION 4.4 Listen again and answer the questions.

1 What is the 'nutty professor' stereotype?
2 What mistakes do intelligent people frequently make at social events?
3 What do intelligent people sometimes do to preserve their reputation?

D SPEAK Work in pairs. Can you think of any counter-arguments or challenges to the three points in Exercise B? Present them to your partner. Use the phrases below to help you.

> First of all, the speaker claimed that ... but ...
> In addition, the speaker stated that ...
> The speaker also mentioned the fact that ...

E SPEAK Work in pairs and discuss the questions.

1 Do you know any intelligent people who behave in the ways that the speaker described?
2 Do you think the speaker has a convincing argument? Why/Why not?
3 The speaker says that intelligence and happiness don't necessarily come together. Do you agree?

VOCABULARY
Thinking

A Complete the questions (1–8) with the correct form of a word or phrase in the box.

> absent-minded common sense curious eccentric eureka moment overthink troubleshoot wishful thinking

1 Are you good at ______________ or do you find it difficult to find and fix problems and faults?
2 Do you sometimes think about the same thing over and over again? Are you ______________ things?
3 Do you solve problems with sudden bursts of inspiration, like a ______________?
4 Do you like to take things apart? Are you ______________ about how things work?
5 Do you make time in the day to organize work? Or does it seem like ______________ ______________ to sit down and plan things?
6 Do you forget where you leave things? Are you ______________?
7 Are you a practical person? Or do you lack ______________?
8 Would you describe yourself as fairly conventional and similar to most people? Or are you a little ______________?

B Go to the Vocabulary Hub on page XVIII.

C SPEAK Work in pairs. Ask and answer the questions in Exercise A. Then decide if your partner is a genius.

PRONUNCIATION

Adding information or changing the topic

4.5 **A** Listen again to the beginning of the debate. Draw arrows to show whether the intonation is rising (↗), falling (↘) or fall-rising (↘↗) at the end of the underlined words/phrases.

Thank you very much. It's an honor to speak against the motion tonight. [1], (__) it's easy to see why so many people believe being intelligent makes your life better. [2]After all, (__) we see intelligent people thriving at school. We see them getting into the colleges they want. We see them graduating with good academic certifications. And [3]on top of that, (__) we see the importance the world gives to certifications.

So, it may seem strange for me to stand here and argue that intelligent people aren't necessarily at an advantage in life. [4]However, (__) that is exactly what I'll do. [5]In fact, (__) there are several clear disadvantages in having a superior intellect.

B SPEAK Work in pairs. Read the dialogues, focusing on the intonation of the underlined words and phrases. Then continue them with your own ideas.

1 **A:** I read that highly-intelligent people frequently like to spend time alone.
B: On top of that, they find it really hard to make friends.

2 **A:** Are you going to watch the debate on intelligence on TV tonight?
B: Yes, I'm planning to. By the way, do you want to go to a debate?

3 **A:** Einstein has been voted the most intelligent person ever.
B: Really? Incidentally, how did you do on your exam?

SPEAKING HUB

A PREPARE Work in groups. Read the motion below and decide whether you will argue for or against it.

Motion: Highly intelligent people should be educated separately.

Order of debate

1 Presentation in support of the motion.
2 Challenge to this presentation.
3 Presentation against the motion.
4 Challenge to this presentation.

B PLAN Decide on the roles each team member will have. Brainstorm arguments to support your position. Try to anticipate the arguments the other team will make, and prepare counter-arguments to them.

C DISCUSS Hold the debate. Follow the order given in Exercise A.

D REFLECT Discuss the following questions:

- How successful was the debate?
- What was your real opinion about the motion?
- Is it difficult to argue for a point of view you don't really agree with?

- Talk about regrets
- Discuss intelligence

Sound and vision

A Work in pairs. Look at pictures a and b and discuss the questions.

1 In picture a, is each half of the circle the same shade of red?

2 In picture b, are the rectangles the same shade of blue?

Turn to **page XXIII** to check your answers.

B 4.6 Listen to two short pieces of music. What colors do they make you think of? Why? Turn to **page XXI** to check your answers.

C Watch the video about an artist. Complete the sentence with the best option.

Neil Haribsson has …

1 partial color blindness in which it is difficult to distinguish between blue and yellow, violet and red, and blue and green.

2 slight color blindness in which it is difficult to distinguish between red, green, brown and orange.

3 total color blindness in which colors are seen as black and white.

Glossary

implant (v) to put an organ, group of cells, or device into the body in a medical operation

sensor (n) a piece of equipment that reacts to physical changes such as the amount of heat or light that exists somewhere

skull (n) the bony case which contains the brain

D Watch the video again. Complete the summary.

Neil Harbisson, an [1] ________, has never been able to see color. He was [2] ________ about color because people always refer to it. He wanted to be able to [3] ________ color rather than to alter his sight. A team of doctors and [4] ________ helped him create an electronic device. This is made up of a color sensor and a [5] ________. The sensor picks up [6] ________ frequencies and the chip [7] ________ the frequency into a sound. Each color creates a different [8] ________.

AUTHENTIC ENGLISH

A Read the sentence from the video and the information in the box. Why do you think Neil's electronic device is compared to something from science fiction?

With the help of a team of engineers and doctors he created something ***straight out of*** *science fiction.*

straight out of

You use *straight out of* to say that something is similar in type to something else. This structure is frequently used to compare the thing we are describing to an imagined or fictional scenario.

B Work in pairs. Complete the sentences in an interesting way.

1 The scenery in Ireland is stunning – straight out of *a travel brochure*.

2 The band is really like *The Beatles*. They sound like something straight out of ________.

3 Himari saw snow for the first time that winter. It was like something straight out of ________.

4 The town has spectacular old buildings, a beautiful lake and no roads. It's straight out of ________.

5 My bag had been stolen, it was pouring rain and I couldn't speak the language. It was straight out of ________.

6 The climb to the summit was long and difficult. It was like something straight out of ________.

C Join with another pair. Compare your answers to Exercise B.

Hearing colors

SAM MALCOLM AMANDA HARRY EMILY

A Work in pairs. Discuss the following questions.

1 What gadgets or devices do you use?
2 Are there any new gadgets or devices you want to buy?
3 Have you ever been to a technology fair or exhibition? Why/Why not?

B Watch the video. Are these sentences true (T), false (F) or not given (NG)?

1 Harry is out sick from work. *T / F / NG*
2 The café was very busy in the morning. *T / F / NG*
3 Emily was about to leave the Tech Fair when a woman approached her. *T / F / NG*
4 The device looked like headphones. *T / F / NG*
5 The first thing that Emily saw on the screen was a red square. *T / F / NG*
6 Emily agrees that Sam should go to the Tech Fair. *T / F / NG*

SPEAKING SKILL

A Work in pairs. Put the following sentences from the video in the order they are spoken.

- ☐ Well, I was at this big Health Tech Fair earlier today, right?
- ☐ But hang on, I'll get to that.
- ☐ Tell me about it. I've had rather a strange one myself.
- ☐ [The woman] asked me to step inside a large box. So I did.
- ☐ [I'm] thinking about heading out when all of the sudden, this woman stops me.
- ☐ Overall it was a strange but unforgettable experience.
- ☐ I was just about to ask her what it was when she slammed the door on me!
- ☐ So I'm standing there saying 'Excuse me … what's going on' and thinking what on earth have I got myself into.

B Match the sentences from the video (1–8) with the strategies (a–d) in the box.

Recounting events

We frequently recount events. To do this effectively we use a number of strategies.

a signaling the start of a story. For example, ___
b giving the background to a story. For example, ___
c evaluating parts of a story. For example, ___, ___
d sequencing events in a story. For example, ___, ___, ___, ___

SPEAKING HUB

A PLAN You are going to tell an interesting anecdote to a partner. You can choose one of the following topics or use your own idea.

- a strange coincidence
- a great event
- an unforgettable trip

B PREPARE Write notes on how you are going to sequence the events in your anecdote.

C DISCUSS Work in pairs. Tell your anecdote. Change roles.

So I'm thinking to myself this is like something straight out of a Hollywood movie.

D REFLECT Work with a new partner and retell them your previous partner's anecdote.

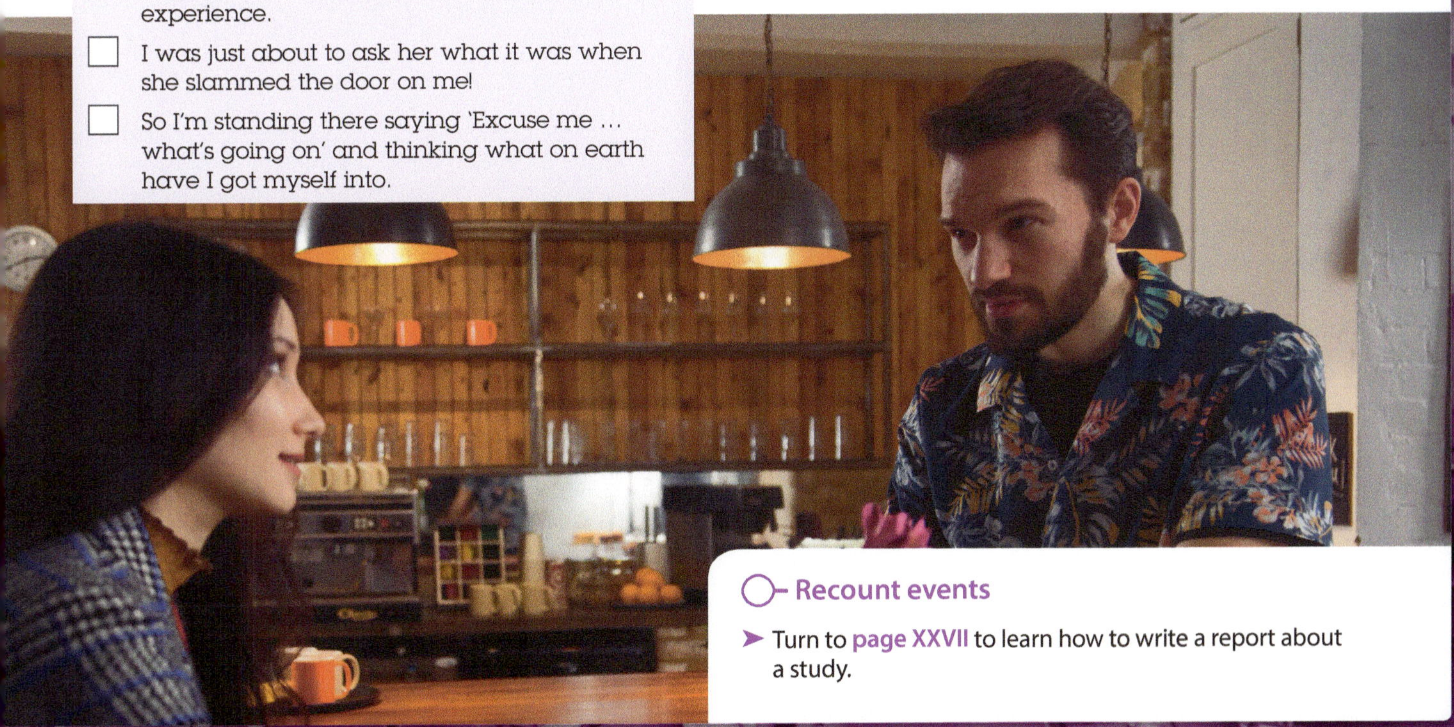

Recount events

➤ Turn to page XXVII to learn how to write a report about a study.

Unit 4 Review

VOCABULARY

A Identify the conceptual metaphor in each sentence. Do you agree with the sentences?

1. If you're not learning something, you're wasting your time.
2. Don't show that you're bright or people will expect big things.
3. Always keep moving, but never go backwards.
4. Invest in your friendships above all else.
5. If you want to win an argument, attack first and attack hard.
6. Keep people in the dark about your goals until you succeed.

B Replace the underlined words in the article with the words in the box. You may need to change the tense of the words.

conclude conduct demonstrate experiment findings hypothesize participants speculate the norm

Pavlovian responses

One of the most famous psychological [1]studies was [2]done by Ivan Pavlov, where the [3]subjects were dogs. Pavlov observed that all dogs naturally salivated whenever they saw food, so he [4]decided this was not a behavior they had to learn.

However, he noticed that his dogs also salivated when his assistant, who frequently fed the dogs, walked into the room. Pavlov [5]guessed that the dogs had learned to associate his assistant with food.

He [6]theorized that the dogs could learn to associate a stimulus with food and would salivate when exposed to this stimulus even when no food was present. He rang a bell whenever he fed his dogs, so that this became [7]typical for them.

After several sessions, he rang the bell when no food was present and his dogs salivated. His [8]results [9]showed that dogs could learn an automatic response to a stimulus.

C Match the sentences (1–8) with the sentences (a–h) that have the same meanings.

1. You're great at troubleshooting.
2. You frequently overthink things.
3. You can be a little absent-minded.
4. You have no common sense.
5. You're a little eccentric.
6. You frequently engage in wishful thinking.
7. You're naturally curious about everything.
8. You frequently have eureka moments.

a. You don't have conventional tastes.
b. You have sudden instances of inspiration.
c. You like learning about things and how they work.
d. You are pretty forgetful.
e. You're not always realistic when you think about future events or situations.
f. You have a tendency to spend too much time considering an issue.
g. You don't understand how to do basic things.
h. You're good at analyzing and solving problems.

GRAMMAR

A Rewrite the beginning of the sentences using the words in parentheses. Then complete the sentences with your own ideas.

1. If all vehicles were automated ... (*Were*)
2. If companies started selling robots to do the housework ... (*Should*)
3. If schools employed robot teachers ... (*Imagine*)
4. If humans could marry robots ... (*Supposing*)
5. If factories hadn't started using robots ... (*Had*)
6. If robots develop conscious thought ... (*Suppose*)

B Choose the correct words to complete the sentences.

1. Jim wishes he ***is / were*** better at sports.
2. If only I ***can / could*** speak three languages.
3. She would love ***have / to have*** a better memory.
4. Tina and Bill wish they ***could save / had saved*** more money as they can't afford their mortgage this month.
5. We should ***not eat / not have eaten*** so much junk food when we were younger.
6. If only I ***have / had*** traveled more.
7. My brother ought to ***spend / have spent*** more time with our parents while they were visiting.
8. I wish I ***can / could*** cook.

5 GAMES

> We do not stop playing because we grow old; we grow old because we stop playing.
>
> Benjamin Franklin

Generation games – a grandma and granddaughter play.

OBJECTIVES

- discuss problem-solving tasks
- discuss gaming and game design
- identify generalizations
- discuss ideas for solving a challenge
- plan a fundraising event
- write a formal report

Work with a partner. Discuss the questions.

1. Look at the picture and read the quote. Why do you think people stop playing games? How does this make us 'grow old'?
2. What games did you like when you were younger? Did you stop playing these games? Why?
3. What games do you like now? Will you keep playing these games when you are older? Will you start any new games?

5.1 21st century games

- Discuss problem-solving tasks
- Discuss gaming and game design

G – the passive voice V – competition and cooperation P – expressing disbelief S – understanding colloquial asides

LISTENING

A SPEAK Read about escape rooms. Do they exist in your country? Are they popular? Why/Why not?

5.1 **B LISTEN FOR GIST** Listen to a conversation between three friends, Lin, Joe and Olga, in an escape room. The conversation is in three parts. Answer the same three questions after each part.

1 Which objects from the pictures did they mention for the first time?
2 Which problem(s) are they trying to solve in this part?
3 What do you think will happen next?

ESCAPE ROOMS

An escape room is a game where a group of people try to escape from a locked room, for example by finding hidden objects, solving clues and working as a team. The idea came from TV shows and computer games with similar problem-solving activities. Escape rooms started in Japan in 2007 and quickly spread around the world. They are popular with children (as venues for birthday parties) and adults (for team-building exercises). There are now over 2,800 escape room venues worldwide.

5.1 **C LISTEN FOR DETAIL** Listen to the whole conversation again. Choose the correct options (a, b or c) to answer the questions.

1 Apart from the metal bar, why can't they get the key out?
   a The cylinder is too deep to reach the bottom.
   b They're worried about breaking the cylinder.
   c The cylinder is too narrow for their arms.
2 How many of the friends have read the instructions?
   a one
   b two
   c three
3 Why can't they use the vase to transfer the oil?
   a It's full of water.
   b It's too big.
   c It can't be moved.
4 Why didn't they notice the message before?
   a The room was too bright.
   b They didn't look in the right direction.
   c They couldn't open the drawer.
5 Why does Joe want to keep playing?
   a He's having too much fun.
   b He's sure they've found all the clues.
   c He thinks people will laugh at him.
6 Why was the towel necessary?
   a Because they needed an accurate measurement.
   b Because the ball was too slippery to hold.
   c Because they needed to weigh it on the scale.

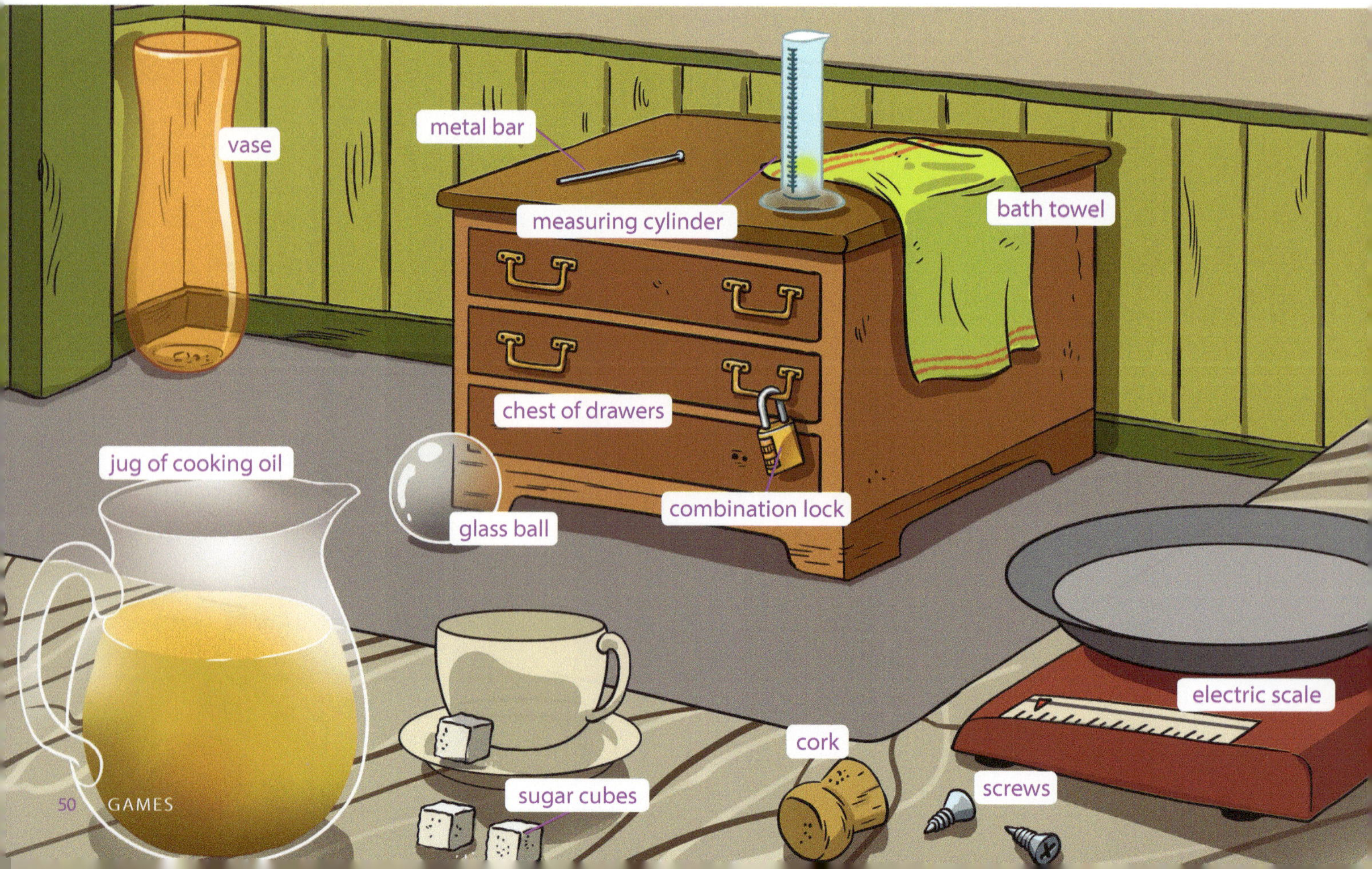

D SPEAK Work in pairs and discuss the questions.

1 How could they have escaped more quickly?
2 Do you think you would have solved all the puzzles?
3 How long would it have taken you to escape from the room?

GRAMMAR
The passive voice

A Look at these sentences from the conversation. Complete the second sentence so that it is in the passive voice.

1 OK, so they've locked us in.
OK, so, *we've been locked in.*
2 Somebody's probably listening to us right now!
__________ right now!
3 Somebody must have written it in fluorescent paint.
__________ in fluorescent paint.
4 They should have given us more clues.
__________ more clues.
5 If we give up now, my friends will make fun of me for weeks.
If we give up now, __________ for weeks.
6 I can't think when somebody's shouting at me!
I can't think when __________!

B Match the sentences (1–5) with the rules (a–d).

The passive voice

a In the structure *make sb do sth*, you need to add *to* in the passive voice (e.g. ___).
b You can make the passive voice from *-ing* forms (e.g. ___) and infinitives (e.g. ___).
c The *get*-passive voice (*get* + past participle) is somewhat informal. Use it to describe unexpected/unwanted events (e.g. ___). It's also useful for distinguishing actions (e.g. *to get married*) from states (e.g. *to be married*).
d Use the causative passive voice (*have/get* + something + past participle) to focus on the person who organizes/pays for a service (e.g. ___) or is the victim of a crime (e.g. *I had my car stolen*).

1 We'll get thrown out if anything gets broken!
2 I don't remember being given any instructions.
3 We were made to sign a form at the front desk.
4 I think the cylinder needs to be filled with water.
5 You need to get your eyes tested!

C Go to the **Grammar Hub** on **page XIV**.

D SPEAK Work in pairs. Ask and answer questions about these topics.

- a way you like/don't like being treated
- a time when you were made to do something
- something you've had done recently/you need to get done soon
- a time when you got lost/stuck/delayed, etc

A: I hate being treated like a child.
B: Really? When do you get treated like that? Who by?

PRONUNCIATION
Expressing disbelief

5.2 **A Match the extracts from the conversation (1–7) with the responses (a–g). Then listen to check.**

1 It's at the bottom of this measuring cylinder.
2 Try pulling it really hard.
3 I wondered what that form was.
4 Should we give up?
5 Something metal? Aha! Two screws.
6 You did it! We're free!
7 There's something in the jug!

a Screws? What are we supposed to do with them?
b Didn't you read it?
c Give up? No way!
d Seriously? That's cheating!
e Yeah right! There's nothing there apart from the oil.
f Really? That was easy!
g Are you joking? We still need to remove the metal bar.

5.3 **B Listen and decide in which sentence (a or b) the speaker is expressing disbelief.**

1 ___ 2 ___ 3 ___ 4 ___

C SPEAK Work in pairs. Take turns to talk about something surprising you did this month. Express disbelief at your partner's statements.

A: I volunteered to teach in India.
B: Really? India? No way!

SPEAKING

DISCUSS Work in small groups. Imagine the room you're in now is an escape room. What clues might help you to escape? Where might those clues be hidden? Express disbelief at each other's suggestions.

READING

A SKIM Look at the picture and the title of the blog post. What do you think urban games are? Skim the blog post to check.

B READ FOR GIST Read the blog post. Which game (a–d) …

1 isn't only played in cities?	___	a	Hidden Bonds
2 teaches you about a place while you play?	___	b	Geocaching
3 has more viewers than live players?	___	c	Pac Manhattan
4 has players who stand out from the crowd?	___	d	Poznan Beyond Time
5 can be confusing to play?	___		
6 takes advantage of a weakness in technology?	___		

URBAN GAMES TURN CITIES INTO PLAYGROUNDS

Glossary

encapsulate (v) to express something in a short clear form that gives the most important facts or ideas

gobble (v) to eat something quickly and usually noisily

It's 6 am and I'm sitting on Trafalgar Square, feeling apprehensive. [1]What on Earth have I let myself in for? The square is virtually empty but I have the distinct feeling I'm being watched by thousands of curious eyes. I receive an SMS: 'Follow the man with the striped umbrella. Don't let him see you.' I spot the man in the distance, jump to my feet and set off in hot pursuit, heart pounding.

I'm playing *Hidden Bonds*, one of the new generation of urban games that are taking off in cities around the world. Urban games encapsulate the best elements of computer games and transfer them to the real world, adding social and physical dimensions to activities that would otherwise involve sitting alone for hours in a darkened room – [2]something I'm all too familiar with!

Urban games originated from a game called *Geocaching*, which uses GPS devices to create virtual treasure hunts. Players are given the GPS coordinates of special boxes called caches, which could be hidden anywhere in the world. Part of the challenge comes from the limitations of GPS, which is only accurate to within a dozen or so meters, so you need to use your eyes. After locating a cache, you win the prize inside – but you must replace it with an appropriate prize for the next player. [3]Sounds amazing, right? … If you're into trudging around muddy fields disoriented and in the middle of nowhere!

One of the best-known modern urban games is *Pac Manhattan*, a version of the arcade game *Pac Man*, played out on the bustling, grid-like streets of New York. [4]How cool is that? Players dressed up as brightly-colored characters from the game race around city blocks, gobbling up virtual 'dots' as they go – and trying to **outmaneuver rival** players to avoid being caught.

Luckily, some urban games are played at a more moderate pace. Visitors to Poznan in Poland can choose from a range of treasure-hunt games to explore the city, while solving clues about the city's cultural heritage and history. For example, in *Poznan Beyond Time*, players embark on a time-traveling adventure to save the world. All you need is a printed game sheet … and some good walking shoes – [5]as I learned through experience!

Then there are games played out for an online audience – which brings me back to *Hidden Bonds*. It's fairly complicated, but in a nutshell, there are four teams, each represented by five 'agents' on the streets of London. The objective is to **cooperate** with your **allies** to **overcome** rival agents, by sending a Bluetooth message to their phone before they can send one to yours. Problem is, the agents have no idea who the other agents are and who's just a normal passer-by, which can lead to some embarrassing moments, [6]I can tell you! The agents receive instructions on their cell phones from 'spymasters', who **coordinate** the players' movements based on the votes of hundreds of 'team members' watching the game live online. The team with the last remaining agent **prevails**.

At a rough estimate, I'd say I've played *Hidden Bonds* as an online team member about 50 times – [7]yeah, sad, I know. **Collaborating** with hundreds of strangers is surprisingly satisfying, but playing live is altogether more exhilarating, especially when you come face-to-face with a rival agent. I managed to catch four opponents before getting caught myself mid-afternoon. Only later did I realize that I'd walked over 20 kilometers in the process! [8]Pretty impressive, right? I'd do it again tomorrow if I could, but there's a seven-month waiting list to participate again as an agent. [9]Just my luck, huh?

C UNDERSTAND ASIDES Look at the asides (1–9) underlined in the blog post. Then answer the questions (a–f). Use the information in the box to help you.

Understanding colloquial asides

Colloquial asides are informal phrases that comment on other information in the text (e.g. *Not bad, huh?*). They frequently take the form of questions or exclamations and they make a text feel more chatty, personal and friendly.

Asides can reveal the writer's personality and attitudes. However, watch out for irony, where the writer means the opposite of what they've written.

Which aside(s) …

- a express(es) genuine enthusiasm? ___ ___
- b is/are likely to be irony? ___
- c suggest(s) the writer feels guilty about their lifestyle? ___ ___
- d show(s) how the writer felt at the beginning? ___
- e suggest(s) the writer frequently describes frustrations in their blog posts? ___
- f hint(s) at problems the writer experienced while playing? ___ ___

D SPEAK Work in pairs and discuss the questions.

1. Which games from the blog post would you like to play? Why?
2. Which would you not want to play? Why?
3. Can you think of any dangers or weaknesses of urban games?
4. Why do you think games like this have become more popular?

VOCABULARY
Competition and cooperation

A Match the words in bold in the blog post with the definitions.

1 ______________ (v) working in partnership
2 ______________ (n) people on the same side as you
3 ______________ (v) wins (e.g. after a long contest)
4 ______________ (v) organize people working together
5 ______________ (v) beat another player or solve a problem
6 ______________ (n) a person competing against you
7 ______________ (v) help/support others

B Go to the Vocabulary Hub on page XVIII.

C SPEAK Work in groups and discuss the questions.

1. Do you prefer games that involve overcoming rivals or cooperating with allies? Think of examples.
2. Think of examples of sports or games where you have to outsmart, outmaneuver, outplay or outrun your opponents.

SPEAKING HUB

A PLAN Work in pairs. Create an urban game for your town/city. Use ideas from the blog post and your own ideas.

B DISCUSS Present your ideas to another pair. Ask and answer questions about how your game ideas will work in practice.

C PREPARE Choose one game idea to develop more fully as a group. Write some simple rules or instructions for your game.

D PRESENT Present your ideas to the class. Which games would you most like to play? Why?

- Discuss problem-solving tasks
- Discuss gaming and game design

5.2 Serious gaming

- Identify generalizations
- Discuss ideas for solving a challenge

G – passive reporting structures
P – *-ate* words
V – reporting verbs; motivation and manipulation
S – distinguishing generalizations from preferred solutions

LISTENING

A SPEAK Work in pairs. Read *The Food Truck problem*. Discuss two or three possible solutions.

B Work in small groups. You are going to think of a solution for three more puzzles. Go to the **Communication Hub** on **page XXII**.

5.4 **C LISTEN FOR SOLUTIONS** Listen to the presentation on Game Theory. What are the correct answers to the puzzles? Use the information in the box to help you.

Distinguishing generalizations from preferred solutions

A speaker frequently presents his or her preferred solution to a problem or puzzle, alongside obvious but problematic solutions or generalizations. Frequently, the generalization is discussed first, before the speaker's preferred solution.

Use the following techniques to distinguish the preferred solution.

- Pay attention to the order in which the speaker presents solutions. Preferred solutions may be presented later.
- Listen for phrases that signal a generalization (e.g. *it seems obvious, you might expect, according to conventional wisdom*).
- Listen for solutions presented with questioning intonation. This may indicate the speaker does not believe this is the correct answer.
- Listen for attitude words like adverbs which can show that the speaker has a skeptical or cautious attitude to a solution (e.g. *presumably, allegedly*).

5.4 **D LISTEN FOR DETAIL** Listen again. Are these sentences true (T) or false (F)? Correct the false sentences.

1. In puzzle A neither participant is likely to win any money. *T / F*
2. Game Theory uses scientific models to find solutions. *T / F*
3. The favorite in talent shows is rarely eliminated in reality. *T / F*
4. The food truck owner in C has no good reason to move. *T / F*
5. The new network would double the amount of traffic. *T / F*

PRONUNCIATION

-ate words

5.5 **A** The suffix *-ate* has two pronunciations. Listen to the extracts from the presentation on Game Theory. Complete the table with the words in the box.

accurate appropriate complicated
cooperate eliminated fascinating

/eɪt/	/ət/

B SPEAK Work in groups . Discuss the following questions.

- Do you prefer games where you have to cooperate with others rather than compete individually?
- What is the most fascinating sporting event you've ever watched?
- Do you prefer playing simple or complicated games?

PUZZLE C:
THE FOOD TRUCK PROBLEM

You decide to open a food truck business.
There's already one other food truck in town, which always parks in the town center (point C).
Where's the best place to park your food truck? You can negotiate with the other food truck owner, if you wish.

VOCABULARY

Reporting verbs

A **Replace the underlined words in each sentence with the correct form of the verbs in the box.**

acknowledge assert conclude imply instruct urge

1. If you share the money, you're <u>saying indirectly</u> that you're willing to cooperate.
2. It's important to <u>say (although it makes my argument weaker)</u> that this strategy doesn't always work.
3. You might <u>decide after thinking carefully</u> that voting for her would be a waste.
4. So I'd <u>strongly advise</u> you to resist the temptation to vote tactically.
5. You should <u>give instructions to</u> the other truck to move to point D.
6. She can simply <u>state as a fact</u> that she's staying in her prime spot.

B Go to the **Vocabulary Hub** on **page XIX**.

C **SPEAK** **Complete the sentences with your own ideas. Then discuss your sentences with a partner.**

- I firmly believe that …
- I'm not sure whether …
- I'm great at …
- Maybe if I'd done … I might not have …
- You really must …

D **Swap partners and report what your previous partner said using reporting verbs.**

GRAMMAR

Passive reporting structures

A **Complete the sentences so they mean the same as the passive voice sentences with *It*.**

1. It can be assumed that your opponent is having the same thoughts.
   Your opponent can be ______________________ having the same thoughts.
2. It is said that Game Theory is one of the hardest branches of mathematics.
   Game Theory is ______________________ one of the hardest branches of mathematics.
3. It's rumored that sports coaches have been experimenting with Game Theory.
   Sports coaches ______________________ have been experimenting with Game Theory.
4. It's expected that she'll win by a landslide.
   ______________________ to win by a landslide.
5. It's reported that this type of thing has happened many times in real life.
   This type of thing ______________________ happened many times in real life.

B **WORK IT OUT** **Complete the rules about passive reporting structures with information from Exercise A.**

Passive reporting structures

Reporting verbs can be used with passive voice structures when we want to introduce a widely held opinion or fact. There are two main ways of doing this.

- ____________ + passive voice + ____________ clause
- ____________ + passive voice + infinitive

Some verbs commonly used with these structures are:

____________, ____________, ____________, ____________ and ____________.

C Go to the **Grammar Hub** on **page XIV**.

D **SPEAK** **Work in pairs and discuss the questions.**

1. When is it useful to use the passive voice to report speech/thoughts?
2. Why do you think 'to rumor' has no active voice form?
3. What's the advantage of using the structure with an infinitive?

SPEAKING

DISCUSS **Work in pairs to think of examples of how Game Theory might be used in sports, business, etc. Use the structure with an infinitive to report generalizations, expectations and assumptions.**

The best time to make an investment is assumed to be when the price is low, but if everyone has the same idea at the same time, then …

READING

A SPEAK What tricks do smartphone games use to keep people playing again and again? Try to think of other situations where these tricks are used.

B SKIM Read *Gamification: treading the line between motivation and manipulation*. Are any situations from Exercise A mentioned?

C READ FOR DETAIL Read the article again. According to the article, are these sentences true (T) or false (F)? Correct the false sentences.

1 Many companies are not yet aware of the potential of gamification. T / F
2 Virtual prizes can still be highly motivating. T / F
3 The majority of people are aware that gamification has been used on them at some point. T / F
4 The major benefit of gamification for charities is that it increases financial donations. T / F
5 Gamification is used to help people recover from injuries. T / F
6 A brand new interactive show is being developed by a production company. T / F
7 Gamification sometimes encourages people to behave in a way that isn't right. T / F
8 The personality of workers may affect how motivating gamification techniques are. T / F

D Work in pairs. Look at the two quotes from Christabel Maware and Lisa Tanaka in the article. Which speaker do you agree with most? Why?

VOCABULARY

Motivation and manipulation

A Match numbers (1–7) with letters (a–g) to form full sentences. Then check by looking for the underlined phrases in the article.

1 As a result of marketing tricks, customers **went**
2 Getting into the college **spurred**
3 People don't mind working hard if you can **tap**
4 If people know *why* they're doing something, they'll be more **inclined** …
5 Gamification can make people **act against** …
6 We offered virtual prizes to **coax** …
7 The online store is designed to **steer** people …

a **to** spend time doing it properly.
b people **into** giving us their data.
c **me on** to study harder for the exams.
d **toward** the most expensive products.
e **nuts for** the new product.
f **their best interests**.
g **into** their natural desire to do a good job.

B Look at the complete sentences in Exercise A. Decide whether the phrases in bold are related to motivation or manipulation.

C Go to the **Vocabulary Hub** on **page XIX**.

D SPEAK Work in pairs. Think of examples from your own experience of each verb in Exercise A. Tell your partner your examples.

My friend tried to coax me into editing her dissertation for her.

SPEAKING HUB

A PREPARE Work in small groups. Choose one of the following challenges, or a similar idea, to solve with your group.

- How to motivate children to read/write more
- How to encourage people to pick up trash

B PLAN Discuss ideas for solving your challenge, using Game Theory and/or gamification techniques.

C PRESENT Present your challenge and solution to the class. Ask and answer questions about how it will work in practice.

D REFLECT Discuss with the class. Which solutions have a chance of becoming popular? Could they make money?

GAMIFICATION

treading the line between MOTIVATION and MANIPULATION

Hitting the treadmill before work, ploughing through deadlines, and finding time to study in the evenings. Maybe these aren't the sort of activities you'd necessarily associate with fun. Yet a glut of apps, websites and online communities that place game-like experiences right at the center of motivation might give you pause for thought. None of this is news for many commercial and public organizations which are already **tapping into** gamification – the application of elements from gameplay psychology to everyday tasks.

Gamification is about more than creating new games for non-gaming contexts. At its heart lies an understanding of the powerful principles that underlie gameplay, the elements that make it so compelling to so many: gratification, competition and rewards. Games increase engagement. Giving people rewards even virtual ones releases dopamine, the feel-good hormone. This leads them to associate that activity or behavior with positive emotions. And that's frequently enough to **spur them on** to repeat it.

The applications of this are diverse: **steering commuters toward** the stairs over the escalator on the Odenplan subway in Sweden by turning them into a giant piano staircase or promoting good learning habits and classroom behavior by giving students 'experience points'. It's highly likely you've experienced gamification yourself, although you probably didn't realize it.

So how can this benefit us? Gamification has made inroads into both the not-for-profit and health sectors. For charities, its greatest potential lies not in fundraising but in fostering a sense of community. If volunteers feel part of an engaged community, they are more **inclined to** stay. Furthermore, they can be incentivized to recruit others or blog about a cause through rewards.

Gamification can also be integrated directly into grassroots campaigning. Hopelab's Zamzee, a physical activity program for families, uses child engagement with technology to improve health. It guides younger users toward doing more physical activity through an activity sensor and a 'physical points' reward system. More specialized healthcare like physical rehabilitation is using and trialing similar approaches. The Medical Interactive Recovery System (Mira) uses a camera to track a patient's physiotherapy movements and translate them into actions within a video game.

Glossary

crave (v) to want something very much and in a way that is very hard to control
incentivize (v) to give someone a reason for wanting to do something
grassroots (adj) relating to or involving ordinary people, especially in politics
plough (v) to finish something that takes a long time and is difficult or boring
recognition (n) praise, respect or admiration

As well as bringing fun to areas where it might be wanting, gamification promises to take fun to the next level in traditional entertainment. Younger and more technologically-savvy viewers may crave an immersive experience, being able to participate in a TV show rather than simply view it. Well, now they can have both their needs for compelling stories and recognition or rewards for their gaming achievements, met at the same time. For example, the popular sci-fi TV show, *Defiance,* by Universal Cable Productions, allowed viewers to shape the plot of television episodes through their actions in an accompanying game.

Some are cautious about gamification, precisely because of its power and how widely it is being used. 'If it can help change our behavior, it can also manipulate us to **act against** our best interests', warns technology lecturer and game designer Christabel Maware. 'I can see it being used very cynically to exploit consumers and employees.' Some companies and organizations have already been called out. For example, a ride-sharing app was criticized for supposedly encouraging drivers to drive further without breaks.

And even where gamification is encouraging 'healthy' competition or making a mundane but necessary work task more appealing, there are concerns around work freedom and surveillance. While leader boards and badges can keep us motivated, having our performance and potentially complex interactions monitored, graded and immediately reported back on by machines sounds more dystopian. 'Simply, not everyone is going to **go nuts for** badges at work', says a Recruitment Manager for AdTech Analytics. For workers who are more introverted or prefer to work privately, this kind of surveillance might be unwelcome and demotivating.

As Lisa Tanaka, founder and CEO of creative agency Gamified International puts it, 'On balance gamification can bring some very positive benefits to many sectors. This stuff works, our brains really are hard-wired for rewards and fun is addictive. We're already being **coaxed into** doing all kinds of things. But with such a powerful tool, there's a pressing need now for companies to be socially responsible in how they use it.'

- Identify generalizations
- Discuss ideas for solving a challenge

Café Hub

5.3 Win or lose

A– *ellipsis* S– **building relationships**

Would you risk it?

a

b

A Work in pairs. What do you think is happening in the pictures (a and b) from the video?

B 00.00–01.00 Watch the first part of a video about an experiment. Answer the questions.

1 What happens if the coin lands on heads?

2 What happens if the coin lands on tails?

Glossary

flip (v) to turn over quickly or to make something turn over
heads (n) the side of a coin that has a picture of a head on it
scenario (n) a situation that could possibly happen
tails (n) the side of a coin that does not have a picture of a person on it

C 01.00–01.30 Watch the second part of the video. Choose the best option (a, b or c) to complete the sentence.

In this situation most people …

a take a risk and maybe win an extra ten pounds or nothing.

b choose the safe option and take fifteen pounds.

c risk it for the chance to win an extra five pounds.

D 01.30–02.20 Work in pairs. Watch the third part of the video and complete the sentences with the correct option.

1 In the second scenario you are given *ten* / *twenty* pounds.

2 You have to choose to accept a safe loss of *five* / *ten* pounds or take a risk.

3 You flip a coin. If it comes up heads, you don't lose anything, but if it comes up tails, you lose *five* / *ten* pounds.

E 02.20–03.27 Watch the last part of the video. What do most people do in the second scenario? Why?

AUTHENTIC ENGLISH

A Work in pairs. Read the sentence from the video and the information in the box. What word has been left out of the sentence?

Would you choose the safe option and get an extra five pounds or take a risk and maybe win an extra ten or nothing?

Ellipsis

Ellipsis is the practice of leaving a word or words out of a sentence when they are not necessary for understanding it. In spoken English, unstressed words are frequently left out at the beginning of sentences if the meaning remains clear.

B Work in pairs. Match the questions (1–6) with the replies (a–f). Then cross out any words which can be omitted from each question and reply.

1 Did you enjoy your vacation?

2 Are you ready yet?

3 Is your dad any better?

4 Are you coming out with us tonight?

5 Did you have any luck with the tickets for the Beyoncé concert?

6 I'm sorry, are you talking to me?

a I'm almost ready. I'm just putting on my makeup.

b Yes, I was asking if you're doing anything nice on the weekend.

c Yes, thanks. He should be out on the weekend.

d No, they were all sold out. It's a shame, really.

e I'm afraid, I can't. I have to work late.

f It was absolutely amazing! Just got back, actually.

C Work in pairs. Take it turns to ask each other short questions from Exercise B and reply with your own short answers.

How sure are you?

SAM MALCOLM AMANDA HARRY EMILY

A Work in pairs. Look at the picture.

1 What board games are popular in your country?

2 Do you ever play them?

B Watch the video. Answer the questions.

1 If Sam and Amanda go in a counter-clockwise direction, which category do they land on?

2 Why does Amanda think Geography is the better option?

3 How does Sam feel about Amanda's strategy?

4 How does Malcolm indicate the correct answer to Sam and Amanda?

5 How does Amanda suggest making the game more interesting?

6 Why doesn't Emily want to take the risk?

7 What's the question Emily and Harry have to answer?

8 What's Malcolm's answer? Is he correct?

SPEAKING SKILL

A Work in pairs. Look at the underlined expression from the video and answer the questions.

1 What is Harry doing?

2 Why do we do this when we're speaking?

Sam: Don't you think it's better to play it safe and go for your strongest categories first … you know … try and build up a lead?

Harry: <u>That sounds like a solid strategy to me</u>.

B Look at the information in the box. Decide which strategy (a or b) is being used in the exchanges (1–4) from the video.

Building relationships

We can build relationships using the following strategies.

a Agreeing with the other person by adding on to what they have said.

b Relating to what the other person has said by evaluating or commenting.

1 Sam: I'm thinking we should go for Geography.

Amanda: Totally … I absolutely hate Geography … it's better to try and get it out of the way earlier.

2 Emily: Ah, good – this is quite hard, I think.

Sam: That is quite tricky.

3 Sam: OK, it can only be one of two countries …

Amanda: … either Finland or Norway.

4 Emily: I mean sport hardly looks like it would be Malcolm's strongest category.

Harry: I guess not but he is smart.

C Work in small groups. Give your opinions on one of the following topics. Use the strategies from Exercise B to build a positive rapport.

- your favorite board game
- your favorite type of movie
- your favorite type of book

SPEAKING HUB

A PLAN Work in small groups. You are going to plan a fundraising event for a local charity. Decide on one of the following.

a dinner a board game evening a yoga class a bake off a fashion show a quiz

B PREPARE Individually think about the preparations for the event. Consider the following points.

- space
- logistics
- timing
- cost

C PRESENT Work in small groups. Decide on a course of action for the event. Try to build up positive relationships and create a consensus.

A: We could hold a banquet dinner at the town hall.

B: Great idea! It could go on all evening.

Plan a fundraising event

➤ Turn to page XXVIII to learn how to write a formal report about gamification.

Unit 5 Review

VOCABULARY

A Complete the instructions with the correct form of a word in the box.

ally collaborate cooperate coordinate overcome prevail rival

Bike clash

The game involves outmaneuvering players on [1]_____________ teams by racing around the city on bikes. Each team has four players, who [2]_____________ with each other, and a 'boss', who [3]_____________ their movements. By [4]_____________ with their [5]_____________, players solve puzzles to identify the times and locations of 'clashes', where they try to [6]_____________ their rivals. When a clash begins, the team with the most players wins a 'trophy'. Any teams that have been outnumbered lose a player. At the end, the team with the most trophies [7]_____________.

B Choose the correct word to complete each sentence.

1. Stores are laid out to ***discourage*** / ***steer*** / ***trigger*** customers toward expensive items.
2. Salespeople try to manipulate us by ***coaxing*** / ***dissuading*** / ***exploiting*** us into spending more than we intended.
3. Loyalty cards can make people ***act*** / ***spur*** / ***tempt*** against their best interests.
4. My sister ***spurred*** / ***influenced*** / ***dissuaded*** me on to enter the race.
5. I wasn't ***exploited*** / ***inclined*** / ***influenced*** to go, but you've persuaded me.
6. Advertising can ***tap*** / ***tempt*** / ***influence*** into people's emotional needs.

C Complete the definitions with the words in the box.

discourage dissuade exploit influence manipulate motivate tempt trigger

1. If you _____________ somebody, you encourage them to want to do something.
2. If you _____________ somebody, you use tricks to convince them do something.
3. If you _____________ somebody from doing something, you persuade them not to do it.
4. If you _____________ somebody from doing something, you encourage them not to do it.
5. If you _____________ somebody, you take advantage of their kindness or naivety.
6. If you _____________ somebody, you offer them something that's hard to resist.
7. If you _____________ somebody's behavior, you change it, maybe without the person noticing.
8. If your actions _____________ a response, they cause it to happen automatically.

GRAMMAR

A Rewrite the sentences so they start or end with the words in parentheses.

1. Somebody must have moved my car. (*my*)
_____________.
2. You can always rely on Leo. (*Leo*)
_____________.
3. I'm worried about somebody seeing me. (*seen*)
_____________.
4. They made us leave our phones outside. (*we*)
_____________.
5. Somebody's going to fix my car. (*I'm*)
_____________.
6. It was nice of them to invite us. (*invited*)
_____________.
7. How did somebody break the vase? (*broken*)
_____________?

B Put the words into the correct order to make sentences.

1. good / considered / my proposal / be / to / enough / wasn't
____
_____________.
2. to / anyone / to the party / expected / hardly / was / come
____
_____________.
3. have / reported / is / hundreds of complaints / received / to / the company
____
_____________.
4. going / at / been / alleged / have / the time / to / the driver / is / too fast
____
_____________.
5. planning / is / a new hospital / to build / rumored / to / the city council / be
____
_____________.
6. been / the kidnappers / have / is / the letter / by / to / believed / written
____
_____________.

Endmatter Contents

Grammar Hub

Vocabulary Hub

Communication Hub

Writing

Grammar Hub

1.1 Nominal clauses

- Nominal clauses function like nouns. They can be used as the subject or object of a sentence, after a preposition, an adjective or the verb *to be*.
- Nominal *-ing* clause (also known as a 'participle clause'):

  Wearing a uniform can help people feel part of the team. (as subject)
  I don't enjoy wearing formal clothes. (as object)
  I'm excited about buying some new outfits. (after a preposition)
- Nominal *that* clause:

  That she won again this year is not surprising. (as subject: this use is rare)
  I explained that she would have to buy a new outfit. (as object)
  I'm worried that I won't fit in. (after an adjective)
- Nominal question clause:

  What you wear is entirely up to you. (as subject)
  My appearance certainly affects how I feel. (as object)
  Fiona felt embarrassed because of how she looked. (after a preposition)
- Nominal infinitive:

  To spend so much money on clothes is totally unnecessary. (as subject: this use is rare)
  It's a good idea to wear dress clothes for an interview. (as object)
  I was surprised to learn about the dress code. (after an adjective)
- We frequently use phrases like *The fact/idea that …* or *The experience/problem of …* to introduce a nominal clause.

  The fact that you got a high grade shows how hard you worked.
  The experience of traveling on the Orient Express was one she would never forget.

Be careful!

- Because *that* clauses and infinitive clauses can sometimes sound unnatural as subjects, we usually use *it* as an empty subject.

  It doesn't surprise me that you hate shopping.
  NOT ~~That you hate shopping doesn't surprise me.~~

1.2 Comparatives and superlatives

- We only use *than* after comparative adjectives and adverbs when it is followed by the thing we are comparing it with.

  CDs are more expensive than they used to be.

Be careful!

CDs are only fractionally more expensive today. NOT ~~CDs are only fractionally more expensive than today.~~

- We don't put *the* before a superlative when we use a determiner.

  Here's our cheapest smartphone.
  NOT ~~Here's our the cheapest smartphone.~~
- To compare things that are the same, we can use *as* + adjective/adverb + *as …*

  Dance music is as popular as it ever was.
- We leave out the second + *as* when the adjective/adverb isn't followed by the thing we're comparing it with.

  None of our audiences have been as large!
  NOT ~~None of our audiences have been as large as!~~
- We can use *the … the* with comparatives to show that two changes are closely connected. As one thing changes, it makes the other thing change.

  The cheaper the technology, the worse quality it is.
  The bigger, the better!
- We can use the structure *more than* with a small number of verbs (*compensate for, double, fulfill, make up for, meet*)

  His enthusiasm and intelligence more than compensated for his lack of experience.
- To show that there is a big difference between two things we can use one of these modifiers before the comparative adjective: *a good/great deal, a lot, considerably, dramatically, far, significantly, much.*

  The new building is considerably bigger than the old one.
- To show that there is a small difference, we use these words and phrases before the comparative adjective: *a little, a fraction, fractionally, marginally, rather, slightly, somewhat.*

  The first movie was fractionally longer than the sequel.
- We can modify superlative adjectives using: *by far, far and away, easily, the very.*

  Tom is by far the smartest boy in the class.
  Tom is the smartest boy by far.
- We can also make a superlative stronger by inserting *possible* after the superlative and before the noun.

  The shopping mall was built in the best possible location.
- We can also use modifiers before the structure *as … as*: *almost, at least, easily, every bit, half, just, twice.*

  My old phone was every bit as good as this new one.

1.1 Nominal clauses

A Correct the mistakes in each sentence.

1 It's an unwritten rule what employees must stick to the dress code.
2 The fact of you wear a uniform sends a certain message about your status.
3 You'll regret not to wear nicer clothes to yesterday's interview.
4 David insisted on that he pay for all the designer clothes I'd chosen!
5 The reason for Sarah's absence that she never received her invitation.
6 That I had forgotten was that the restaurant only lets in nicely dressed customers.
7 The clothing company more than double its annual profits.
8 Sandra always wants to buy clothes at the possible lowest price.

B Choose the correct options to complete the conversation.

Joey: I'm really eager [1]*to start* / *about starting* my new job next week.
Phoebe: I'm sure [2]*you to* / *that you will* fit in really well.
Joey: They explained [3]*that they have* / *having* a dress code there. So … [4]*that I buy* / *buying* a business suit is my first priority! Will you come and help me choose one?
Phoebe: Of course. I think you should be prepared [5]*to spend* / *that you spend* a lot of money.
Joey: What do you mean?
Phoebe: You must know [6]*that* / *the fact* an expensive suit will last longer than a cheap one?
Joey: Oh, I see [7]*what* / *that* you mean. OK. But [8]*I'm needing to know* / *what I really need to know* is what color to choose!

C Complete the second sentence so that it has a similar meaning to the first sentence, using the word given. Write between two and five words.

1 That designer clothes are hugely expensive is well-known.
FACT
______________________ designer clothes are hugely expensive is well-known.
2 It's none of my business what he does in his free time.
SPENDS
______________________ his free time is none of my business.
3 The purchase of expensive school uniforms is a problem which many parents face.
OF
Many parents face ______________________ ______________ expensive school uniforms.

➤ Go back to page 3.

1.2 Comparatives and superlatives

A Choose the correct options to complete the sentences.

1 Thank goodness I have tech-savvy friends like you – you're ______________________.
a the best b the best friend
2 I think we need to replace our company logo with something ______________________.
a funkier than b funkier
3 Winning the Young Tech Designer of the Year was ______________________ ____________ moment!
a the my proudest b my proudest
4 Your handwriting is ______________________ Carol. Well done!
a the neatest handwriting b the neatest
5 We've redesigned our website so that it's ______________________.
a more user-friendly b user-friendlier
6 CDs weren't around for very long, and CD burners disappeared almost ______________________.
a as quickly b as quickly as

B Write one word in each blank to complete the sentences.

1 My sister is a great ________ more concerned about appearances than I am.
2 A tailored jacket is ________ and away the most important item of clothing in your closet.
3 I dress ________ fraction more informally on Fridays, but I don't feel comfortable in casual clothes.
4 In my opinion, having the right image is every ________ as important as saying the right thing.
5 Chelsea only ever buys the ________ best in terms of clothing and accessories.

C Complete the sentences using a word from the box and your own ideas.

considerably	half	marginally	twice

1 The green dress costs $25. The blue dress costs $27.
The blue dress costs ______________________.
2 My sister is a fashion vlogger and earns ten times more than I do!
My sister earns ______________________.
3 We were expecting 100 people at the fashion show, but only 50 came.
Only ______________________ we expected came to the fashion show.
4 I believe that you have to do double the work of others to be sure of success.
I believe that you have to work ______________________.

➤ Go back to page 7.

Grammar Hub

2.1 Narrative tenses

	Active Voice	Passive Voice
Simple past	**I realized** it was a great idea.	**We were given** a month to finish the job.
Past progressive	**We were hoping** for a better result.	**The plans were being drawn up** at the time.
Past perfect	**They had already bought** the site.	**The architects had been chosen.**
Past perfect progressive	**We had been walking** for hours.	

- We use the simple past in a story or narrative to explain the main events.

  *We **met** on Saturday, outside Victoria train station.*
- We use the past progressive to describe the background to a story, actions in progress at a particular point or together with the simple past, to describe actions or situations that were interrupted by shorter events.

  *The sun was shining when Amy **left** the house.*
- We use the past perfect to show that one event happened before the other.

  *He **had waited** for over an hour by the time she finally arrived.*
- We usually use the past perfect progressive together with the simple past, for actions that were in progress before another action in the past.

  *I **had been working** all day so I **decided** not to go out that night.*
- We can use the simple past with *did* + base form for emphasis.

  *He **did** look very anxious when he left.*

Be careful!

- We don't usually use the passive voice form of past perfect progressive.

  Someone had been watching us. NOT *~~We had been being watched.~~*

2.2 Future in the past

	Future in the past
Past progressive	We **were traveling** to Australia the next day.
was/were going to	Sam **was going to start** looking for another job.
would + base form	I thought it **would be** nice to take a gift.
was/were + infinitive	Jody **was to contact** me as soon as her plane landed.
was/were + perfect infinitive	Jody **was to have contacted** me as soon as her plane landed.
was/were about to + base form	We **were about to leave** the house when the phone rang.

- When we are talking about the past, we sometimes need to talk about things that had not yet happened. We can use the past progressive or *was/were going to* for this.

  *When I saw her, she **was leaving** the next day.*

  *Jim **was going to** meet Mary that evening.*
- We can use the past form of *will* (*would*).

  *That discovery **would turn** out to be important later on.*
- We can also use past forms of the verb *be* with the infinitive or the perfect infinitive. The infinitive can be used for events that came true or didn't come true.

  *He **was to deliver** the report on Tuesday. (And he did.)*

  *He **was to deliver** the report on Tuesday. (But he failed.)*

  The perfect infinitive is usually only used for events that didn't come true.

  *He **was to have delivered** the report on Tuesday. (But he failed.)*
- We can also use past forms of *be* + *supposed to* + base form or perfect infinitive. These are often, but not always, used for events that didn't come true.

  *He **was supposed to have delivered** the report on Tuesday. (But he failed.)*

  *He **wasn't supposed to look** at the files. (But he did anyway.)*
- To describe something that was going to happen soon, we use the past form of the verb *be* with the word *about*. Sometimes we add the word *just*.

  *She had her coat on because she **was (just) about to take** the dog for a walk.*

Be careful!

- You may need to make other changes to pronouns, times, places, etc, in the same way as you do in reported speech.

  Anna was leaving for Canada the following day. NOT *~~Anna was leaving for Canada tomorrow.~~*

2.1 Narrative tenses

A Choose the option in each sentence that is <u>NOT</u> correct.

1 I ___ what he meant.
 a had finally been understanding
 b finally understood
 c had finally understood

2 ___ to wait in the reception area.
 a They told me
 b I was telling
 c I was told

3 Jim had been swimming earlier and his hair ___ wet.
 a was
 b had got
 c was getting

4 Angie was shocked by what she ___ at the film festival.
 a had seen
 b saw
 c has seen

5 He had gotten the job but he ___ the starting date.
 a hadn't been being told
 b wasn't told
 c hadn't been told

6 It was a terrible day and it ___ heavily.
 a was raining
 b had been raining
 c had been rained

B Correct the underlined mistakes. Sometimes more than one answer is possible.

1 I realized I <u>left</u> my money at home.
2 When I looked out of the window, I saw that it <u>rained</u>.
3 I <u>did to realize</u> that I had forgotten my keys before I left.
4 Janine changed her mind about the theater but it was too late as I <u>already bought</u> the tickets.
5 We arrived a little early and we <u>told</u> to wait until the manager was free.
6 Greg went to see the doctor because he <u>wasn't being feeling</u> well.
7 As soon as we had finished the discussion, we <u>had left</u>.

C Complete each sentence with the correct form of the verb in parentheses, active voice or passive voice. Sometimes more than one answer is possible.

1 I was angry because ______________ (*I / keep*) waiting for an hour.
2 The sun was shining and the birds ______________ (*sing*) in the trees.
3 The reason I was tired was that I ______________ (*have to / walk*) all the way home.
4 We ______________ (*only / work*) on the project for a week when it was canceled.
5 Pete ______________ (*not / tell*) about the change of plans so he knew nothing.
6 We couldn't use the living room because it ______________ (*decorate*).

➤ Go back to page 17.

2.2 Future in the past

A Choose the correct options to complete the sentences.

1 I couldn't go to the party because I ***would take / was taking*** a test the next day.
2 When we were at school together, he was ***becoming / going to become*** a doctor.
3 They thought it ***will / would*** be fun to play a trick on us.
4 Our new TV was to have been ***delivered / delivering*** yesterday but it didn't come.
5 I was ***about / about to*** ask him where he got the money when he made an excuse and left.
6 When the movie was released, few people thought it ***would be / was being*** a success.
7 The fingerprints found at the scene of the crime ***were being / were to be*** vital in solving it.
8 Thinking there was no way he ***was going / would*** to get into college, he didn't even apply.

B Write one word in each blank to complete the sentences.

1 Sonja ______________ about to get on the train when she realized she'd left her ticket at home.
2 Philippe couldn't believe he was actually ______________ to graduate in three weeks' time.
3 We all knew it ______________ be fun to enter the competition.
4 Both girls truly believed they ______________ going to be famous one day.
5 At that point it dawned on me that London ______________ to be my new home.
6 Marie was ______________ about to give in her report when she spotted the mistake.

➤ Go back to page 21.

Grammar Hub

3.1 Future structures

- We can use a variety of grammatical forms to express the future, such as future forms with *will*, the simple present, the present progressive and *be going to*.

  They'll plant some more trees over the next few weeks.
  When does the presentation begin?
  I'm going to install solar panels on my roof.
- We use the future progressive (*will be* + *-ing*) to describe a situation that will be in progress at a particular point in the future.

  Scientists will be making an important announcement at 3 pm.
- We use the future perfect (*will have* + past participle) to describe changes that will be completed before a particular point in the future.

  He will have fixed the air-conditioning by the end of the day.
- We can use the future perfect with adverbs in the middle position after *will*.

  *Pollution in our city will **surely** have impacted quality of life by the end of the next decade.*
- We use the future perfect progressive (*will have been* + *-ing*) to focus on the future results of an earlier future process, and/or to measure the length of time of that process.

  The crew will have been tearing down the old factory for twelve weeks by the end of June.

Be careful!

- We usually don't use *will* after words which signal conditional sentences such as *if*, *unless*, *when*, *while*. So we use present progressive instead of future progressive, and present perfect instead of future perfect.

  She'll be hanging up flyers while I'm meeting with the council. NOT ~~*She'll be hanging up flyers while I'll be meeting with the council.*~~

- We can use a modal verb such as *may*, *might* or *could* instead of *will* in these future structures to express possibility.

  They'll be switching to renewable energy soon. (= definitely)
  They could be switching to renewable energy soon. (= it's possible)
- We also use phrases such as *be on the verge of* + *-ing*, *be on the brink of* + *-ing*, *be due to* + base form, *be set to* + base form, and *be about to* + base form to refer to the future.

  *Danielle **was on the verge of achieving** her goal.*

3.2 Negative inversion

- We use negative inversion when we want to emphasize a negative element of a sentence. We place the negative element at the beginning and we invert (= swap over) the subject and auxiliary verb.

  *I have never seen such waste in my life. = **Never have I seen** such waste in my life.*
  *I'm not saying we need to leave now. = **By no means am I saying** we need to leave now.*
  ***No way could I ever drive** a gas-powered car again.*
- We add *do*, *does* or *did* in inverted clauses when there is no auxiliary verb.

  *She never received an apology. = Never **did** she receive an apology.*
- We use *than* after the phrase *no sooner*.

  *No sooner had she written the document **than** her computer crashed.*
- Inversion is often used with the structure *not only … but also*.

  Not only did I meet the mayor, but I also met the governor.
- Some words and phrases change in inversions, and negative verbs become positive.

  ***Nobody** told me about that once. → Not once did **anybody** tell me about that.*
  *You **must not** say that under **any** circumstances. → Under **no** circumstances **must** you say that.*
  ***That's not** the only solution by **any** means. → By **no** means **is that** the only solution.*

- There are also some inversions which do not contain negative words and phrases. These include sentences which start with *only* for time expressions, such as *Only after*, *Only when*, *Only once*, *Only if*, *Only by*, *Only rarely*, and *Rarely*, *Hardly* and *Barely*.

  Only by reading the instructions three times did I understand what to do.

Be careful!

- With some inversions, such as *No sooner … than*, *Not only*, *Hardly*, etc, it's the first verb and the subject which inverts.

  *Not only **was he late**, he was also unprepared.*
  *Hardly **had we sat down** when the fire alarm went off.*
- With other inversions, such as *Only after*, *Not until*, etc, it's the verb in the main clause which inverts.

  *Only after I'd arrived **did I realize** I'd gotten the day wrong.*
  *Not until he'd spent hours online **did he find** a suitable photo.*

- We don't use inversion when the negative word or phrase is the subject.

  None of my colleagues take public transportation. NOT ~~*None of my colleagues do take public transportation.*~~
- The verb and subject invert after *neither* and *nor*.

  *None of their staff knew the answer, and **neither did we**.*
  *I haven't told anyone, and **nor has Jake**.*

3.1 Future structures

A Match the statements (1–7) with their purposes (a–g).

1 We're going to build a zero-emissions home. ___
2 I'll call the manager, if you like. ___
3 I think you'll be famous someday! ___
4 When are they going to close down that factory? ___
5 The talk begins at 10 am. ___
6 I think I'll just take the bus instead. ___
7 With all these clouds, it's going to rain very soon! ___

a making a prediction from strong evidence
b explaining plans
c talking about a fixed scheduled event
d making a prediction based on opinion more than evidence
e making an offer
f asking about plans
g making a decision while speaking

B Choose the correct options to complete the sentences.

1 We'll *be testing* / *have tested* the new equipment for a few hours tomorrow.
2 They'll have *been laying* / *laid* the foundation by the end of next week.
3 I'll *be meeting* / *have met* Jim later today, if you'd like to join us.
4 Will you have *be working* / *been working* with the company for very long when you retire?
5 The company will have *built* / *been building* two new hotels by the end of the year.
6 They won't *have taken* / *be taking* questions from the audience after the talk.
7 By the time she finishes the marathon, Kayla will have *jogged* / *been jogging* for six hours.
8 He'll probably still be working unless he *decides* / *will decide* to leave it for next week.

C Complete the second sentence so that it has a similar meaning to the first sentence. Use between two and five words, including the word in bold.

1 Thirty minutes from now, the meeting will conclude. **DUE**
The meeting ______________________ conclude in half an hour.
2 The scientists will make the discovery any day now. **VERGE**
The scientists are ______________________ the discovery.
3 In less than a minute, the rocket will launch. **ABOUT**
The rocket ______________________ launched.
4 The two companies are close to sealing the deal. **BRINK**
The two companies ______________________ sealing the deal.
5 By the end of the year, the agreement will have expired. **SET**
The agreement is ______________________ by year's end.
6 I'll be collecting samples and she'll be recording them. **WHILE**
She'll be recording samples ______________________ them.

➤ Go back to page 26.

3.2 Negative inversion

A Rewrite the sentences (1–6) using inversion and the words given.

1 Nobody asked me if I passed my driving test.
Not once ____.
2 I'd just arrived home when they called me back to the office.
No sooner ____.
3 We seldom see players with such natural ability.
Rarely ____.
4 He is really smart and incredibly funny.
Not only ____.
5 Tina realized her purse had been stolen when she went to pay her bill.
Only when ____.
6 You must not open that door.
Under no circumstances ____.

B Write one word in each blank.

Anna was in charge of organizing her company's annual conference. She had met the manager a week before to make the plans, and no [1]______________ had they sat down to talk than the manager was called away. She waited forty-five minutes, and [2]______________ until she got up to leave did the manager re-appear. On the day of the conference, [3]______________ no means did everything go according to plan. Not [4]______________ was the turnout low, but she [5]______________ had trouble with the conference venue. [6]______________ in a million years would she have thought things could go so wrong.

➤ Go back to page 31.

Grammar Hub

4.1 Conditionals without *if*

We can use inversions to replace the word *if* in some conditional sentences.

- In first conditional sentences, we can use *should* to replace *if*.

  __Should__ you have any questions, please don't hesitate to call. (= If you have ... OR If you should have ...)
- In second conditional sentences, we can use *were* to replace *if*.

  __Were__ it banned, there would be an outcry. (= If it were banned...)

  __Were__ I to do the quiz, I'm sure I would win! (= If I were to do ...)
- In third conditional sentences, we can use *had* to replace *if*. This use of inversion is more common in formal language.

  Had he used a brain training game, he would have remembered more. (= If he had used ...)
- We can also sometimes use verbs, *-ing*, past participles and the imperative in place of *if*.

Imagine / Suppose (that)	**Suppose** (that) I had a chip in my brain, would I be smarter?
Assuming / Supposing / Presuming / Providing (that)	**Assuming** (that) you complete the experiment, will you have all the data? **Providing** (that) we didn't make any mistakes, the results should be correct.
Provided (that)	**Provided** (that) you believe in yourself, you will definitely succeed.
Imperative ... , and	**Read** more books, **and** you will improve your memory.

Be careful!

- With the imperative and *Imagine/Suppose (that)*, you cannot swap the clauses around.

  Imagine you were offered a brain implant, would you want it?

  NOT ~~Would you want a brain implant imagine you were offered it?~~

4.2 Wishes and regrets

wish / if only + simple past/progressive	to wish that the present was different	**I wish / If only I didn't blush** so easily.
wish / if only + could/would		**I wish / If only I could stop** stammering. **I wish / If only you would speak** more clearly.
wish / if only + past perfect simple/progressive	to wish that the past was different	**I wish / If only I had participated** in the study.
wish / if only + could have + past participle		**I wish / If only I could have participated** in the study.
ought (not) to / should (not) have + past participle *ought (not) to / should (not) have been + -ing*		**I shouldn't have gazed** at the floor all the time!

- *If only* often sounds more dramatic or emphatic than *wish*. It can be used about other people, but usually suggests the speaker's opinion.

  __If only__ David had known the answer! (= I wish David had known the answer!)
- To be more formal, we use *were* instead of *was* after *I/he/she/it*.

  If only I __were__ more confident.

  He wishes he __were__ more confident.
- When you want to talk about your own wishes, use *could* instead of *would*.

  I wish I __could__ speak Chinese. NOT ~~I wish I would speak Chinese.~~
- We can also use *ought to have* + past participle to talk about things that were ideal or desired in the past.

  They __ought to have managed__ the meeting better.
- We can use *would love to have* + past participle to talk about regrets.

  I __would love to have had__ enough time to explain my views. (= I didn't have enough time and that's a shame.)
- We can also use *if* + past perfect simple + modal verbs (subordinate clause) and modal verb + *have* + past participle to talk about imagined situations in the past with regret.

  I __could have learned__ more, __if I had prepared__ for the classes.

4.1 Conditionals without *if*

A Complete each second sentence so it means the same as the one before it.

1 If I had dropped my coffee on her carpet, I would have felt embarrassed!
Had ______________________________, I would have felt embarrassed!

2 If brain implants were available to everyone, I would definitely get one!
Should ______________________________, I would definitely get one!

3 If you practiced Sudoku puzzles more, you would get better at them.
Were ______________________________, you would get better at them.

4 If you become dizzy after taking the medication, please contact your doctor.
Should ______________________________, please contact your doctor.

B Choose the correct options to complete the sentences.

1 ***Imagine*** / ***Imagining*** that you met Elon Musk, what would you say to him?

2 ***Suppose*** / ***Providing*** that we didn't make any errors during the experiment, the data should be correct.

3 ***Look*** / ***Suppose we look*** at the problem from a different angle, we might be able to find a solution.

4 ***Imagine*** / ***Assuming*** that she told us the truth, I think we can conclude that she's innocent.

5 ***Supposing*** / ***Provided*** all the participants had been men, would that have made a difference to the results?

6 ***Conducting*** / ***Conduct*** more research, and you will have a clearer picture.

C Complete the sentences with the correct form of the verbs in parentheses.

1 ______________ (*act*) confidently, and you will never again feel embarrassed.

2 Suppose you ______________ (*arrive*) late for an exam, what would you do?

3 Provided that you think before you speak, you ______________ (*not say*) anything silly.

4 Were I ______________ (*say*) the wrong thing, I would apologize.

5 Assuming you ______________ (*prove*) he was cheating, would you tell the examiner?

6 Should AI become a reality, we ______________ (*need*) to improve human intelligence.

7 ______________ (*I know*) that the research was unethical, I would never have taken part in it.

8 Unless the government ______________ (*increase*) funding for the program, the researchers will never be able to complete their study.

➤ Go back to page 41.

4.2 Wishes and regrets

A Choose the correct options to complete the sentences.

1 I wish I had made a better first impression. = I ***made*** / ***didn't make*** a good impression.

2 I wish I could understand what the lecturer was saying. = I ***understand*** / ***don't understand***.

3 You shouldn't have been so clumsy! = You ***were*** / ***weren't*** clumsy.

4 Helena wishes her new boss was more friendly. = Her new boss ***is*** / ***isn't*** friendly.

5 I would love to have taken part in the experiment. = I ***took*** / ***didn't take*** part.

6 You ought not to have worn that eccentric outfit. = You ***wore*** / ***didn't wear*** an eccentric outfit.

7 If only I didn't feel so socially awkward. = I ***feel*** / ***don't feel*** socially awkward.

8 If only he could express himself more clearly. = He ***is*** / ***isn't*** able to express himself clearly.

B Complete the sentences with the correct form of the verbs in parentheses.

1 I wish I ______________ (*prepare*) more thoroughly for my interview yesterday.

2 If only I ______________ (*know*) whether or not I got the job!

3 I wish I ______________ (*can / get*) her autograph but I wasn't brave enough.

4 If only I ______________ (*not / say*) that I'm disorganized!

5 I wish I ______________ (*can / think*) clearly under pressure but I get so stressed.

6 I wish I ______________ (*not / have to*) go through job interviews!

C Correct the mistakes in each sentence.

1 You shouldn't have copy your essay from the internet.

2 The girls wish they was on vacation.

3 You could had told me the truth – I would have believed you!

4 I would love to had taken part in the research.

5 The scientists ought to have make their findings public.

6 Gemma doesn't wish she was so shy.

7 If only I hadn't get embarrassed with new people.

8 I could have done better, if I haven't been so nervous.

➤ Go back to page 43.

Grammar Hub

5.1 The passive voice

	Passive voice
make sb do sth	We **were made to wait** for over an hour.
Passive voice with *-ing*	I hate **being kept** waiting.
Passive voice with infinitive	He would like **to be given** the chance to retake the test.
get passive voice (informal)	They **got thrown** off the course.
Causative *have* and *get*	I need to **have** my phone **serviced.**

- Remember that we use the passive voice when we don't say who or what causes the action (usually because the person or thing is not known, not important or not obvious).

  *We **were made to take** the exam again. NOT ~~We were made by the examination board to take the exam again.~~*
- We use *by* when we know who does/did an action and we want to mention it.

  *I don't mind being told **by my boss** to work late but I don't like it when I have to cover for other people.*
- We can use an infinitive or *-ing* passive voice form, depending on the verb or construction that comes before it. Some verbs can be followed by an infinitive or *-ing* with no or little change in meaning. Prepositions are always followed by *-ing*.

  *We arranged **to be** paid in cash.*
  *I appreciated **being** told about the delay.*
  *The child loved **to be / being** thrown up in the air.*
  *Johnny never talks about **being** thrown out of college.*
- We use the causative (in any tense) when someone does something for us, or when we are victims of a crime or accident. The causative with *have* is more formal than the causative with *get*.

  *I **got** my hair cut. OR I **had** my wallet stolen on the train.*
- We can use *get* + object + past participle when we talk about causing something to happen or be done by somebody else.

  She is popular because she gets things done.
  They are angry because they are not getting their packages delivered on time.
- We can also use *get* + object + *-ing* to talk about causing someone or something to do something.

  The book on game theory got Susan thinking.

Be careful!

- In both the *get* passive voice and the causative, *get* is usually less formal than *have*. Don't use it in formal situations.

  The letter asked us when we had had the house built. NOT ~~The letter asked us when we had got the house built.~~

5.2 Passive voice reporting structures

- Some verbs, such as *allege*, *assume*, *believe*, *expect*, *know*, *say*, *report*, *rumor*, *suppose*, *understand*, are often used in the passive voice as reporting verbs. The verb *rumor* can only be used in this way.
- We frequently use the impersonal *it* with these verbs.

  ***It** is rumored that the President will announce her resignation today. (= There is a rumor that ...)*
- With an impersonal *it* passive voice, we can follow the reporting verb with either an infinitive or *that*.

  *It is understood **to be** a complicated situation.*
  *It is understood **that** the situation is complicated.*
- With a personal reporting structure, beginning with *I/you/he/she/it/we/they*, we use the past participle of the reporting verb, followed by infinitive.

infinitive	He **is known to be** a thief.
progressive infinitive	She **is thought to be planning** a comeback.
perfect infinitive	They **are rumored to have started** a secret mission.
perfect progressive infinitive	They **are believed to have been watching** us.

- We can sometimes use modal verbs before the reporting verb.

  *It **can** be assumed that the business is still profitable.*
- In both personal and impersonal constructions, we can use the reporting verb in the past if we are referring to something people *expected/knew/thought*, etc. However, if the action was done in the past, and we are reporting it now, the verbs must reflect this.

  *He **was** known to be hiding.*
  *It **was** thought that they **had failed**.*
  *He **is** understood to **have made** contact.*
  *It **is** believed that he **discovered** America.*

Be careful!

- Do not use *that* in a personal passive voice (one that begins with *I/You/He/She*, etc).

  He is rumored to be planning to make cuts. NOT ~~He is rumored that he is planning to make cuts.~~

5.1 The passive voice

A Find the mistakes and correct them. Some sentences are correct.

1. I was made to fill in pages of details on the form.
2. I dislike to be spoken to as if I don't understand anything.
3. He looks forward to be spoiled when he visits his family.
4. In my school, we used to get told off for the slightest things.
5. You look different – have you had your hair done?
6. Do you know what we were made do in the intelligence test?

B Complete the sentences with the correct *-ing* or infinitive passive voice form of the verb in parentheses.

1. I miss ____________ spend summer vacation days on the beach. (*be able to*)
2. Justine begged ____________ for the things she'd said in anger. (*forgive*)
3. The taller kids tended ____________ for basketball, regardless of their ability. (*choose*)
4. The manager wouldn't tolerate ____________ with. (*disagree*)
5. Paul didn't mention ____________ by the police – do you think he's hiding something? (*stop*)
6. He couldn't remember ____________ onto an elephant, although he had the photo to prove it had happened. (*lift*)

C Complete the sentences in the passive voice or causative form.

1. Active: They made him sign the document.
   Passive: He ____________.
2. Active: If you're not careful, they'll throw you out.
   Passive: If you're not careful, you'll ____________ ____________.
3. Active: I'd like to know how much it costs for you to clean my car professionally.
   Causative: I'd like to know how much it costs to ____________.
4. Active: How on earth are we going to find someone to repair that window on a Sunday?
   Causative: How on earth are we going to get ____________?
5. Active: I'm sure they didn't tell me to be here half an hour early.
   Passive: I don't remember ____________ ____________.
6. Active: Someone will steal your car if you leave it there.
   Causative: You'll get ____________ ____________.

➤ Go back to page 51.

5.2 Passive reporting structures

A Choose the correct options to complete the sentences.

1. We are supposed *to be* / *to be being* there at nine o'clock.
2. It is rumored *to be* / *that* the company is having difficulty.
3. Two members of staff are alleged to *transfer* / *have transferred* money into private accounts.
4. It *is* / *was* originally thought that they were related.
5. They are believed to *plan* / *be planning* a trip overseas.
6. The police are known to *be* / *have been* following him recently.
7. It was thought that there *was* / *to be* a secret tunnel, but nothing has been found.
8. On her first day, *it* / *she* was expected to write three reports.

B Complete the text with a suitable form of the verbs in the box.

announce discuss focus look make plan

Director disputes

Home Articles About us Contact

Following tomorrow's meeting, Collins is expected [1] ____________ his resignation. The company is thought [2] ____________ to specialize in the near future. They are expected [3] ____________ on only one product, and Collins is known [4] ____________ his objections to this very clear on several occasions in the past. Although Collins is understood [5] ____________ the situation with top management for several weeks, the company is now rumored [6] ____________ for a way to force him out.

C Rewrite the sentences using both personal and impersonal passive voice structures. Use the reporting verb in bold.

1. People **believe** he is very rich.
   He ____________.
   It ____________.
2. Some people **report** that he was awarded over one million dollars.
   He ____________.
   It ____________.
3. They **say** she knows her subject inside out.
   She ____________.
   It ____________.
4. Critics **claim** that the game's story is too complex.
   The game ____________.
   It ____________.
5. Many **think** that it is a complex problem.
   The problem ____________.
   It ____________.
6. People **assume** she is shy but she's just quiet.
   She is ____________.
   It is ____________.

➤ Go back to page 55.

Vocabulary Hub

1.1 Clothes and fashion

A Choose the correct word to complete the sentences.

1 There is a ***dress code*** / ***uniform*** at my work – for example, we aren't allowed to wear torn jeans or shorts.

2 Many people try to copy Audrey Hepburn's style – she was a real trend ***setter*** / ***follower***.

3 The theme of the party is *Superheroes* – everybody has to wear a(n) ***outfit*** / ***costume***.

4 You need a new pair of pants – those are so old and ***scruffy*** / ***casual***.

5 People who work in fashion usually dress boldly to ***fit in with*** / ***stand out from*** the crowd.

6 I like ***baggy*** / ***oversized*** clothes in the summer because they keep you cool.

B Work in pairs. Look again at both options in Exercise A. What is the difference between each option? What do they have common?

➤ Go back to page 2.

1.2 Experimenting with prefixes and suffixes

Add the correct prefix or suffix from the box to the words in bold to complete the sentences.

friendly ish prone proof re resistant savvy super

1 It doesn't matter if he dropped the camera in the pool – it's **water**__________ and **shock**__________.

2 She's really up-to-date with new recording and video equipment. She's very **tech**__________.

3 The sound quality is awful and it looks like it was made at home. It's just too **amateur**__________ to be taken seriously.

4 She has a lot of experience making vlogs. She has every reason to feel __________**confident** about her abilities.

5 He's always breaking the stuff on the set. I guess he's just **accident**__________.

6 The themes on the show are too adult. I couldn't show my children that – it's not **family**__________.

7 You've made a mess of that video. You'll have to __________**start** it.

➤ Go back to page 9.

2.1 Describing art

Choose the correct words to complete the sentences. Then discuss the sentences with your partner. Do you agree?

1 Some people enjoy looking around galleries, but I find it very ***tedious*** / ***unconventional***.

2 Some modern theater is incredibly ***pretentious*** / ***groundbreaking*** – it's more about making the writer feel smart than actually saying anything important.

3 Art needs to be ***hilarious*** / ***thought-provoking***. Without a deeper meaning, it's just a pretty picture.

4 Some of the most ***iconic*** / ***sensational*** photographs can be disappointing when you see them up close.

5 When a writer uses the same idea in his or her work too many times, it feels really ***repetitive*** / ***overrated***.

➤ Go back to page 14.

2.2 Compound adjectives

Make compound adjectives with the words in the box to complete the sentences. Use each word only once.

highly late open part self thick well world

1 I work for a company now, but, in the future, I'd like to be ________________**-employed**.
2 Traveling can introduce you to new ways of seeing the world and make you more ________________**-minded**.
3 Sandra's looking for a ________________**-time** job so she can study and work at the same time.
4 Sometimes as a writer you need to be ________________**-skinned** – you can't take criticism personally.
5 Rob is a ________________**-motivated** person who loves his job and wants to excel at it.
6 It's important that my job is ________________**-paid**, so I have some disposable income after I pay all my bills.
7 He is definitely a celebrity in his own country, but he isn't ________________**-famous** yet.
8 There is a ________________**-night** convenience store below our apartment that will be open.

➤ Go back to page 20.

3.1 Sustainability

Complete the text with the words in the box.

biodegradable consume emission exploitation neutral offsetting renewable

Home Articles About Contact

How to be green

1 ________________ energy from sun, wind, rain and waves is one possible solution to the environmental problems we face today. It helps us to address the over-2 ________________ of natural resources that are finite like minerals, oil, natural gas and coal. Some businesses and organizations aim to be carbon-3 ________________ by 4 ________________ the amount of carbon they release. There are even some zero-5 ________________ buildings which actually create as much energy as they 6 ________________. Also using 7 ________________ materials, for example, in food packaging, is another important step because these materials break down naturally and cause less waste.

➤ Go back to page 26.

3.2 Verb–noun collocations

Cross out the incorrect word or phrase in each group.

1 We managed to ***achieve*** / ***attain*** / ***deliver*** / ***perform*** / ***meet*** our goals.
2 We have made ***a concerted effort*** / ***limited progress*** / ***reasonable headway*** / ***advances in the right direction*** / ***room for improvement***.
3 They performed ***impressively*** / ***particularly*** / ***reasonably*** / ***relatively*** / ***surprisingly*** poorly.
4 The statistics ***demonstrated*** / ***hindered*** / ***displayed*** / ***showed*** a marked imbalance.
5 We should set ***significant progress*** / ***realistic goals*** / ***clear objectives*** / ***measurable targets***.
6 We have seen ***little movement*** / ***a deadline*** / ***a new record*** / ***regression*** / ***incremental progress***.

➤ Go back to page 33.

4.2 Science and research

Choose the correct word to complete the sentences.

1 What are some examples of social ***findings*** / ***norms*** in your social group?
2 Can you ***conduct*** / ***speculate*** how most people would react if they were publicly told they had a low score on a test?
3 Do you think the study above proved the theory that the researchers ***demonstrated*** / ***hypothesized***?
4 What did this study ***conduct*** / ***demonstrate***?
5 Can you think of another idea for ***an experiment*** / ***some findings*** to prove the hypothesis?
6 Is it important to read the ***findings*** / ***participants*** of a study to understand the conclusions?
7 Have you ever ***conducted*** /***speculated*** an experiment at school or college?
8 What have you ***concluded*** / ***conducted*** about embarrassment by reading the texts?

➤ Go back to page 43.

4.2 Thinking

Choose the correct options to complete the sentences.

1 While she is very smart, she just isn't very practical. She doesn't have much ***common sense*** / ***wishful thinking***.
2 I was lying on the beach when I had an amazing idea for my business – it was a ***eccentric*** / ***eureka*** moment.
3 He is very ***eccentric*** / ***absent-minded*** – he really stands out from the crowd and doesn't mind doing things in his own unique way.
4 I'd say I'm a little ***curious*** / ***absent-minded*** – for example, I left my key card at home this morning and couldn't get into my office.
5 If you make a resolution but put no effort into planning how to achieve it, then your idea is just ***wishful thinking*** / ***common sense***.
6 We need someone who can analyze and solve serious problems – in other words, ***troubleshooting*** / ***overthinking*** skills are essential for this job.
7 Lara always ***troubleshoots*** /***overthinks*** things; sometimes she should just follow her instincts.
8 Tim describes himself as ***curious*** / ***eccentric***, but I would describe him as nosy.

➤ Go back to page 44.

5.1 Competition and cooperation

A **Read the definition of *outmaneuver*. What does the prefix *out-* mean?**

outmaneuver – definition and synonyms
VERB Pronunciation /ˌaʊtməˈnuːvə(r)/
to defeat or gain an advantage over someone by being more smart or skillful than they are

B **Complete the sentences with the correct form of the verbs in the box.**

outdo outnumber outplay outrun outsmart outweigh

1 You'll need to be fast to ________________ your rivals and win the race.
2 When we played tennis, she completely ________________ me, and I lost every game.
3 It's not perfect, but on balance, the advantages ________________ the disadvantages.
4 When I bought a new car, my neighbor didn't want to be ________________, so he bought one too!
5 I managed to ________________ my opponent by solving the clues faster.
6 In my class, women ________________ men by three to one.

➤ Go back to page 53.

5.2 Reporting verbs

Complete the second sentences with a reporting verb from the box and reported speech.

alleged boasted clarified doubted speculated

1 'The new bridge is supposed to reduce traffic congestion, but I don't think it will.'
Daniel ______________ whether the new bridge ______________________________ traffic congestion.

2 'Sorry – I think you misunderstood me. I didn't offer to do all the work for you.'
Tania ______________ that ______________________________ for me.

3 'Who knows? If you'd studied harder, you might have gotten a better grade.'
Max ______________ that I ______________________________ harder.

4 'I was awesome at the Take or Share game! I made over $200!'
Victoria ______________ that ______________________________ Take or Share game.

5 'I can't prove it, but I know that Andy lied on his résumé to get the job.'
Michael ______________ that ______________________________ to get the job.

➤ Go back to page 55.

5.2 Motivation and manipulation

Complete the text with the correct form of the phrases in the box.

act coax go nuts inclined spur steer tap into

A day in the life of... a salesman

I wouldn't say my job involved [1]______________ people into buying things that they don't actually want. I would never convince someone to buy a faulty product or [2]______________ against their best interests. But I totally believe in the quality of our products – they have been well-designed and [3]______________ what the market really wants. My job is just to [4]______________ people toward the most appropriate products in our range to meet their needs. To be honest it's not difficult. The products sell themselves. Customers are [5]______________ for them. It is the quality of the product that [6]______________ me on to do my job as well as I can. If the product is no good, you're not [7]______________ to make the same effort to sell it.

➤ Go back to page 56.

Communication Hub

2.2 Students A and B

Read what your answers to the quiz say about you.

ARE YOU CUT OUT FOR FAME?

MOSTLY 1S
You have a very clear vision for your future and nothing will stop you from achieving it. You welcome negative feedback as a way to improve and grow as a person. You want to be well-known, even if this won't necessarily make you rich.

MOSTLY 3S
You feel comfortable among large groups of people and don't need a lot of alone time. That being said, you would not particularly enjoy your private life being discussed online. You are fairly ambitious and would like to be respected in your field. But you also have other interests in your life which are important to you. Fame might not be for you.

MOSTLY 5S
You don't enjoy being the center of attention and value privacy. For you, work is a small part of your life, secondary to spending time with friends and family. The purpose of working is to earn money to do the things you enjoy. Fame isn't for you.

➤ Go back to page 20.

4.1 Students A and B

BRAIN TEASERS

Try these fun brain teasers to keep your mind active and increase your intelligence.

1 If you were running in a marathon and you passed the person in third place, what place would you be in now?

2 An electric train is moving north at 100 kph and a wind is blowing to the west at 10 kph. Which way does the smoke blow?

3 If there are six apples and you take away four, how many do you have?

4 I'm tall when I'm young and I'm short when I'm old. What am I?

Answers: 1 Third 2 An electric train doesn't produce smoke. 3 Four 4 A candle

➤ Go back to page 38.

4.3 Students

Low frequency sounds, like number 1, are connected to earthy tones like browns and reds. High frequency sounds like, number 2, are connected to violet tones like blue and purple.

➤ Go back to page 46.

4.1 Student A

Using your own words, explain each situation to your partner. Then decide what you would do in pairs.

Situation 1

Imagine that a company begins selling brain implants. They allow you to learn and remember information quickly. For example, some people use them to learn languages or other skills instantly. However, the implants have also caused people to lose some of their memories. Would you buy one?

Situation 2

Imagine that a company begins selling highly advanced robots. These robots will take on any tasks that you need them to do, provide companionship for people who live alone, and protect you and your house. They are also smart enough to learn and use their initiative. Would you get one of these robots?

Situation 3

Imagine that artificial intelligence is used for both medical check-ups and treatment in the future. The AI has a higher rate of accurate diagnoses than human doctors. You have the choice between a human doctor or an artificial intelligence system. Which would you pick?

➤ Go back to page 41.

4.2 Students A and B

Think of a time when you did something you regret. Use the prompts below or your own ideas. Discuss it with your partner.

- You failed a test.
- You forgot something.
- You lost something.
- You missed an appointment.
- You sent an email or message to the wrong person.
- You wore the wrong type of clothes.

➤ Go back to page 43.

5.2 Students

Work in small groups to solve the puzzles.

PUZZLE A: THE TAKE OR SHARE IT GAME

You and a stranger are both offered a choice: **TAKE** or **SHARE**.

If only one player chooses **TAKE**, they keep $1000.

If both players choose **SHARE**, they get $500 each.

But if both players choose **TAKE**, they get nothing.

You can't communicate with each other.

What's the best strategy if you play once?

What if you play multiple times?

PUZZLE B: THE TALENT SHOW DILEMMA

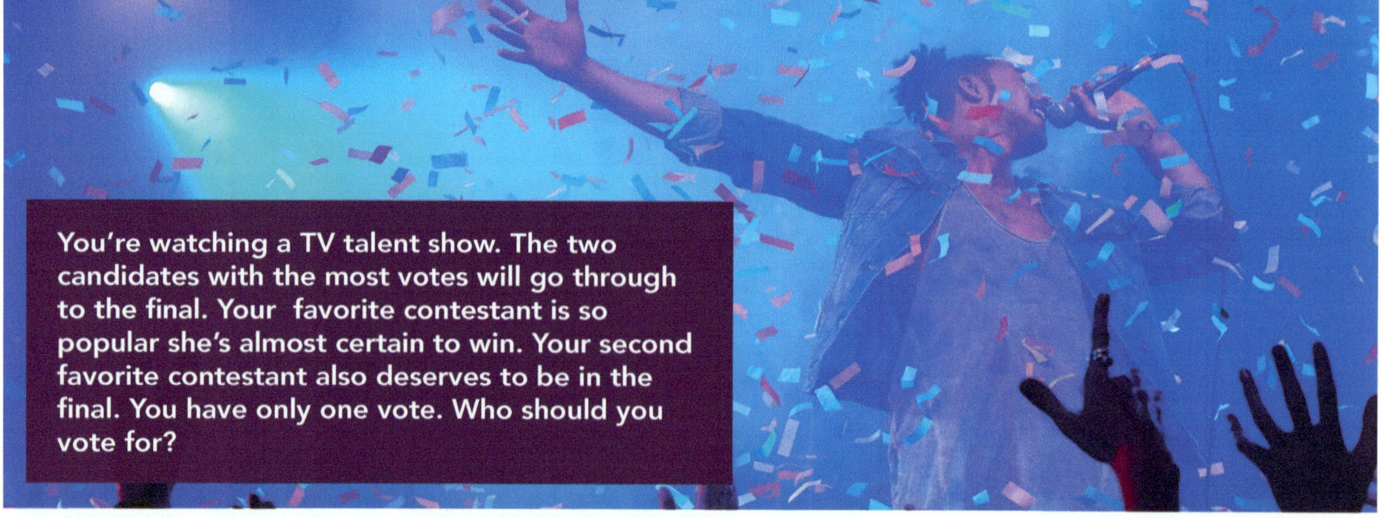

You're watching a TV talent show. The two candidates with the most votes will go through to the final. Your favorite contestant is so popular she's almost certain to win. Your second favorite contestant also deserves to be in the final. You have only one vote. Who should you vote for?

PUZZLE D: THE ROAD NETWORK

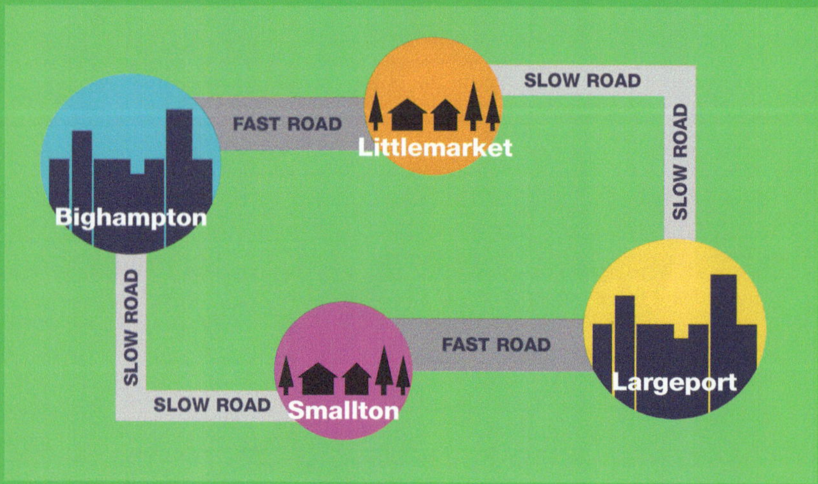

The map shows the road network between four towns. Where (if anywhere) should you build a new road to solve the towns' traffic problems?

➤ Go back to page 54.

4.3 Students

Both pictures are brightness illusions known as Munker's illusion. Although the shapes appear to vary in brightness, they are actually the same. It is the colors next to them that make them appear different.

➤ Go back to page 46.

3.2 Student B

Read the situation and prepare what you will say.

You're being interviewed for a radio program about progress. You feel that while there have been a lot of advances, overall life in the modern world is getting worse. You can think about the following points or use your own ideas to prepare:

- the impact of technology
- community
- quality of life
- cost of living
- employment
- the environment

Complain to the interviewer about how life is getting worse in the modern world.

➤ Go back to page 31.

4.1 Student B

Using your own words, explain each situation to your partner. Then decide what you would do in pairs.

Situation 1

Imagine that a company begins selling body upgrades. You can use its technology to make you stronger, faster and more skillful. People can use the upgrades to fix their sight and hearing, or repair injuries. However, the new parts don't look natural, so it will be clear you have had upgrades. Would you use this service?

Situation 2

Imagine that a company begins offering a memory back-up service. You can download the memories from your brain onto its servers and then view the memories whenever you want. You can also share selected memories with others. However, you don't get to choose which memories are downloaded. Everything has to be downloaded together. Would you use this service?

Situation 3

Imagine that a highly advanced robot in the future demanded the same rights as a human. The robot argues that it is as conscious as a human being. Would you support the demands of the robot?

➤ Go back to page 41.

W— making your blog post successful

A Look at the buttons. What do you think *skeuomorphism* means?

B Read *4 things you need to know about skeuomorphism*. Complete the article with the headings (a–d).

- **a** Is skeuomorphism cool?
- **b** Is skeuomorphism useful?
- **c** What are some examples of skeuomorphism in real life?
- **d** What is skeuomorphism?

4 things you need to know about SKEUOMORPHISM

Have you ever wondered why the best websites look fresher and smarter than yours? Do you want to learn the powerful secret of great web design? Then you need to know about skeuomorphism.

1 ___

Here's a simple definition: skeuomorphism involves making digital objects look like things in the real world. The earliest websites just had a lot of text. Instead of a 'click here' button, you simply had the words 'click here'. But web designers soon realized that users prefer life-like buttons and switches.

2 ___

Examples of skeuomorphism are everywhere. Is there a trash can on your phone for 'delete'? A cogwheel for 'settings'? An envelope for 'messages'? The list of examples is endless. Skeuomorphism even brings outdated technologies – like floppy disks and sand-filled hourglasses – back to life.

3 ___

It depends. Early web designers got carried away with skeuomorphism. Every button had a 3D appearance, with shadows and reflections. This led to a backlash in the early 2010s called 'flat design', which gave a cleaner, less fussy appearance. Flat design managed to appear both retro and modern … but also a little boring.

4 ___

Yes and no. Skeuomorphism does make things more user-friendly and intuitive. We all know that a green phone means 'start a call' and a red one means 'end a call', but what if you've never seen an old-fashioned phone? What if you're color-blind? By all means use skeuomorphism in your web design, but don't assume your users can work out what everything means!

Want to learn more about web design trends? Click here to sign up for our online course.

C SPEAK Work in pairs. Discuss the questions in the headings.

D Match the objectives (1–3) with the strategies (a–g).

Making your blog post successful

A successful blog post achieves three objectives:

1 People will find it using search engines. ___, ___, ___, ___

2 They will read it from start to finish. ___, ___

3 They will take some action that helps the writer. ___

- **a** Include a number in your title (i.e. 7, not seven). Search engines prefer them!
- **b** End with a clear call to action (CTA), e.g. 'sign up for our newsletter'.
- **c** Ask questions in your first paragraph, but only answer them later in your blog post.
- **d** Choose one key word or phrase and use it as many times as possible in your blog post.
- **e** Use questions as section headings. Many people use questions to search.
- **f** Speak to readers as 'you' and offer to solve their problems.
- **g** Include a lot of common search terms like 'definition' and 'examples'.

E Find examples of the strategies (a–g) in the blog post.

WRITING

A PREPARE Work in groups. You are going to write a blog post about a trend or trends in general. Think of ideas for topics.

B PLAN Choose your key word or phrase (to be repeated many times in your blog post), your title and a series of questions to use as section headings.

C WRITE Write your blog post. Make sure the first paragraph encourages the reader to keep going to the CTA!

D REVIEW Read some other people's blog posts. Use the box above to evaluate the posts.

W– writing concisely

A Read this announcement and answer the questions.

Reviews wanted

Have you recently read a classic book or watched a classic movie? We're starting a series of reviews of classic books and movies and we want your opinions.
Is the book or movie as good as everyone says it is? Is it still relevant today? Please send us a review for the college paper. Write 220–260 words.

1 What should be reviewed?
2 What questions should be addressed by the review?
3 Who is the target audience?
4 How long should the review be?

B Read the review. Does the writer agree that the book deserves its reputation as a classic? Which parts of the review tell you this?

Alice's Adventures in Wonderland

1 Fantasy children's novel *Alice's Adventures in Wonderland* was published in 1865. The book, adapted for movies and television and translated into over 100 languages, fully deserves its reputation as a classic and is just as fun today as it always was.

2 At the beginning of the story, Alice sees a white rabbit wearing clothes and talking to himself. Following the rabbit, she falls down a hole into a bizarre world of strange and wonderful creatures, including a snooty caterpillar and the mysterious, grinning Cheshire Cat.

3 One of the reasons that *Alice's Adventures in Wonderland* is so popular is that it is a nonsense story. It's not a typical linear story or a story with logic and a moral. It's about the strange situations and unusual characters created by the author, and they surprise and delight readers.

4 Another reason for the book's enduring popularity is Lewis Carroll's playful use of language. The story is full of riddles, puzzles, puns and made-up words. One of the most famous examples is the 'unbirthday party' at the Mad Hatter's tea party.

5 *Alice's Adventures in Wonderland* is without a doubt a classic book that has captured the imaginations of generations of children and adults. Its creative story, characters and playful use of language make it a unique story – and one that everybody should read at least once.

C Look at the review and identify which paragraph contains the following information.

a an overall opinion of the work and a recommendation ___
b key information about the work and a general opinion of it ___
c analysis of a second positive or negative aspect of the work ___
d a plot summary or description of the work ___
e analysis of one positive or negative aspect of the work ___

D Read the review again and answer the questions.

1 Which characters from the book are mentioned?

___

2 How is the story of this book different to most other books?

___

3 What example of playful use of language does the writer give?

___

E Find features of concise description in the text. Use the information in the box to help you.

Writing concisely

If you need to write concisely, you can use some of the following features:

- noun phrases: *English writer and mathematician Charles Dodgson*
- reduced adjective clauses: *Charles Dodgson, writer and mathematician, published his first book.*
- participle clauses: *Educated at home, Dodgson wrote poems and short stories.*

WRITING

A PREPARE Look again at the announcement in Exercise A.

B PLAN Plan your review. Use your answers to question 2 in Exercise A to help you.

C WRITE Write your review. Use your plan to help you.

D REVIEW Exchange your review with a partner. Do you have similar information? Underline any information that you don't think is correct.

E EDIT Read your partner's comments. Rewrite any parts you think should change.

Write a persuasive email

W– persuasive techniques

A SPEAK Read the email. Who is the writer? Who is he writing to? Why?

To: Lakeside residential estate (group)
From: Daniel Hernandez
Subject: Road resurfacing

Dear all

a As you know, the internal roads in our neighborhood are in dreadful condition. Not only does this look ugly, but it also damages our cars. Furthermore, one of our loved ones may be injured by tripping on the uneven surface.

b With that in mind, the housing association has set aside funds to resurface the roads. As I'm sure you remember, the roads were last resurfaced five years ago. One option is simply to use the same cheap materials again (and in five years, the surface will have deteriorated again).

c I would like to propose an alternative: self-repairing concrete. Thanks to cutting-edge technology, self-repairing concrete is infused with billions of tiny limestone-producing bacteria, *Bacillus pseudofirmus*. While sealed in concrete, these bacteria remain inert, but when exposed to air they multiply rapidly. No sooner does a crack appear in the concrete than millions of these bacteria will wake up and plug the crack.

d As you can imagine, although self-repairing concrete is somewhat expensive, it will save us money in the long run (see attached calculations). More importantly, if one serious accident can be prevented over the next five years, I'm sure you'll agree it will have been worth the extra cost.

e I know you are all smart people, so let's make the smart decision. Please support my proposal at our next housing association meeting.

Best regards

Daniel

B Read the email again. Match the questions (1–5) with the paragraphs (a–e). Then discuss the questions in pairs.

1 What is a potential objection and how can it be overcome? ___
2 What is the most likely solution and what's wrong with it? ___
3 What action does the reader need to take? ___
4 What is the problem and why should the reader care? ___
5 What's an alternative solution and why is it better? ___

C Underline examples of each technique in Daniel's email. Use the information in the box to help you.

Persuasive techniques

1 Use words like *we, our* and *let's* to build a connection with the readers.
2 Flatter your readers by claiming they're intelligent and knowledgeable.
3 Provide facts and figures to support your claims, in an attachment if appropriate.
4 Use emotive language and imagery to appeal to your readers' fear of loss, damage or injury.
5 Explain technical issues in simple language, but include some impressive technical terms.
6 Use *although* or *while* to link weaknesses with strengths.

D Work in pairs. Use the techniques in Exercise C to make these email extracts more persuasive.

1 Your biggest problem is that you spend too much money on electricity.
2 Please support me so I can solve this problem for you.
3 The road surface is so bad that delivery drivers may refuse to drive into our neighborhood.
4 I admit this solution will be extremely disruptive during the building work.

WRITING

A PREPARE Work in groups. You are going to write a persuasive email about sustainability, smart materials or voluntourism. Generate a list of ideas. Use the following questions to help you:

1 What problem are you trying to solve?
2 Who do you need to persuade?
3 What do you want your reader to do?

B PLAN Plan a five-paragraph email. You can use the five questions from Exercise B to help you.

C WRITE Write your email, using techniques from this lesson.

D REVIEW Exchange your email with a partner. Do you use similar techniques? Comment on how the email could be made more persuasive and underline any mistakes.

E EDIT Read your partner's comments. Rewrite any parts you think should change.

W— hedging

A Study the list of twenty words for one minute. Then try to write them all down.

experiment brilliant eccentric
participant professor memory
argument common sense fashion
metaphor trend brainpower website
conclusion project world-famous
iconic obstacle self-portrait
inspiration

B Work in groups. Compare the words that you remembered. Which words did most people remember?

C Read the report. Which words did the study find were more likely to be recalled? Why were these words more likely to be recalled?

INVESTIGATING SHORT-TERM AND LONG-TERM MEMORY

Introduction

This report describes an experiment to replicate the results of an earlier study. Murdock (1962) investigated the concepts of short-term and long-term memory by getting students to memorize a list of words. He found that students were more likely to recall the words at the beginning and end of the list. [a]He concluded that this **may** be because the words from the beginning of the list were stored in the long-term memory, whereas the words at the end of the list were stored in the short-term memory.

Methods

Thirty participants (16 men and 14 women) were asked to look at a list of 20 words for a minute. They were then asked to try to recall the words.

The words that participants wrote down were analyzed to see which words were recalled the most and if the position of the word in the list affected the students' ability to recall the word.

Results

The results confirmed Murdock's findings and showed that students were more likely to recall words from the beginning and end of the list.

Discussion

Murdock suggested that students studied the words at the beginning of the list more carefully, maybe by saying the words out loud. [b]**He believed that** this meant that the words had been processed enough to enter the long-term memory. [c]The words at the end of the list were the words students had just looked at, so these were **likely** to be stored in the short-term memory. [d]This study replicated Murdock's findings and **suggests** that his theory may be correct.

Conclusion

It can be concluded that when given information as a list, we are more likely to recall items from the beginning and end of the list.

D Look at the report again and match the report headings with the descriptions (1–5).

1 Analysis of the meaning of the findings ______
2 Description of participants and what was done ______
3 The findings ______
4 A summary of the outcome ______
5 An overview and background information ______

E Match the rules with the four sentences (a–d) in the report.

Hedging

In a scientific report unless something is a well-established fact, we should use hedging to make our claims less strong and less open to criticism. Use:

1 auxiliary verbs such as *may*, *might* and *could*: ___
2 adverbs such as *probably*, *possibly* and *likely*: ___
3 verbs that that allow for some doubt, such as *seem*, *appear*, *suggest*, *indicate*: ___
4 introductory phrases to qualify, such as *We believe*, *We understand*, *In our view*: ___

WRITING

A PREPARE Read about a similar experiment. Imagine you have recently replicated this experiment.

B WRITE Write a full report about it.

Glanzer and Cunitz (1966) did a similar experiment to Murdock, but they had two different groups. One group received the test immediately after looking at the words. The other group had a 30-second delay before they did the test and had to count backwards in threes from 99 during the delay. The results showed that although participants could recall the words from the start of the list, they could not recall the words from the end of the list. Glanzer and Cunitz concluded that this was because these words were no longer in participants' short-term memories because of the delay and the distraction.

References

Glanzer, M, & Cunitz, A R (1966) 'Two storage mechanisms in free recall' *Journal of Verbal Learning and Verbal Behavior*, 5(4), 351–360.

W– using depersonalization

A Read the report and answer the questions.

1. Who commissioned the report? Why?
2. What worked well in the two case studies? What went wrong?
3. Which elements does the writer recommend copying? What would the writer change?

Using games to attract tourists to Littlemarket

Background

At a recent meeting of the Littlemarket Tourism Board, [1]it was proposed that an investigation should be conducted into the use of urban gaming and gamification to attract tourists. This report summarizes the research and provides a series of recommendations.

Case study 1: Bighampton

Two years ago, the tourism board in Bighampton launched a series of treasure-hunt worksheets for tourists, which [2]were reported to be enjoyable by 55% of participants. However, they were found to be too easy by 25%. The games were moderately successful in attracting tourists to some lesser known attractions, but the overall impact on tourist numbers was minimal (a 1.5% rise).

Case study 2: Smallton

Last year, the Smallton Tourism Board developed an app to gamify tourists' experience of the town. Badges could be won for visiting particular cafés, museums and other attractions. [3]In spite of widespread frustration with technical problems, the results were impressive, with some cafés and restaurants reporting an 80% increase in sales. [4]It remains to be seen how successful the app has been at boosting overall tourist numbers, but initial indications are positive.

Recommendations

[5]It would be relatively cheap and simple to develop a series of printable treasure hunt maps. Ideally, a range of levels (beginner to expert) would be offered. However, [6]it would be necessary to invest significantly in marketing [7]to raise awareness of the games. [8]It would also make sense to use the gamification techniques from Smallton's experiment to encourage tourists to spend more money. Unlike Smallton, we should involve local businesses in the costs of developing and promoting our games.

The costs of developing an app are currently beyond our budget, so I recommend gaining experience first with a cheaper, low-tech solution and then, if appropriate, upgrading to a sophisticated technical solution in two to three years.

B Complete the examples with the extracts (1–7) from the report.

Using depersonalization

Depersonalization involves removing people from your writing to make it more formal. Depersonalization techniques include:

- **a** *it* + *be* + adjective + infinitive: *we could cheaply and easily* → ___; *we'd need to* → ___
- **b** preposition + noun: *Although many people got frustrated* → ___
- **c** changing verbs into nouns or adjectives: *55% of participants said they had enjoyed* → ___; *to inform people about* → ___
- **d** the passive voice: *somebody proposed that* → ___
- **e** other impersonal phrases: *We still don't know* → ___; *we should also* → ___

WRITING

A PREPARE Work in groups. You have been asked to write a report for a language school about using games to attract new students and improve language skills. Discuss how escape rooms, urban games, game theory or gamification could help your language school.

B PLAN Imagine two or three case studies involving other language schools. Write notes about each case study in your plan.

C WRITE Write your report. Use depersonalization techniques to make it suitably formal.

D REVIEW Exchange your report with a partner. Do you use similar techniques? Comment on how your partner has used depersonalization.

E EDIT Read your partner's comments. Rewrite any parts you think should change.

Irregular Verbs

Base form	Simple past	Past participle
be	was/were	been
become	became	become
begin	began	begun
break	broke	broken
bring	brought	brought
build	built	built
buy	bought	bought
can	could	(been able to)
catch	caught	caught
choose	chose	chosen
come	came	come
cost	cost	cost
cut	cut	cut
do	did	done
drink	drank	drunk
eat	ate	eaten
fall	fell	fallen
feel	felt	felt
find	found	found
forget	forgot	forgotten
get	got	got
give	gave	given
go	went	gone/been
grow	grew	grown
have	had	had
hear	heard	heard
hit	hit	hit
hold	held	held
hurt	hurt	hurt
keep	kept	kept
know	knew	known
leave	left	left
lend	lent	lent

Base form	Simple past	Past participle
let	let	let
lose	lost	lost
make	made	made
mean	meant	meant
meet	met	met
must	had to	(had to)
pay	paid	paid
put	put	put
read	read	read
ride	rode	ridden
run	ran	run
say	said	said
see	saw	seen
sell	sold	sold
set	set	set
shut	shut	shut
sing	sang	sung
sit	sat	sat
sleep	slept	slept
speak	spoke	spoken
spell	spelled	spelled
spend	spent	spent
stand	stood	stood
steal	stole	stolen
take	took	taken
teach	taught	taught
tell	told	told
think	thought	thought
throw	threw	thrown
understand	understood	understood
wear	wore	worn
win	won	won
write	wrote	written

PHONETIC SYMBOLS											
Single vowels			Diphthongs			Consonants					
/ɪ/	fish	/fɪʃ/	/uw/	new	/nuw/	/p/	pen	/pen/	/s/	snake	/sneɪk/
/iː/	bean	/biːn/	/eɪ/	face	/feɪs/	/b/	bag	/bæg/	/z/	zoo	/zuː/
/ʊ/	foot	/fʊt/	/ɔɪ/	boy	/bɔɪ/	/t/	tea	/tiː/	/ʃ/	shop	/ʃɒp/
/uː/	shoe	/ʃuː/	/oʊ/	nose	/noʊz/	/d/	dog	/dɒg/	/ʒ/	television	/'telɪvɪʒən/
/e/	egg	/eg/	/ju/	use	/juz/	/ʧ/	chip	/ʧɪp/	/m/	map	/mæp/
/ə/	mother	/'mʌðər/	/aɪ/	eye	/aɪ/	/ʤ/	jazz	/ʤæz/	/n/	name	/neɪm/
/ɜː/	word	/wɜːrd/	/aʊ/	mouth	/maʊθ/	/k/	cake	/keɪk/	/ŋ/	ring	/rɪŋ/
/ɔː/	talk	/tɔːk/				/g/	girl	/gɜːrl/	/h/	house	/haʊs/
/æ/	back	/bæk/				/f/	film	/fɪlm/	/l/	leg	/leg/
/ʌ/	bus	/bʌs/				/v/	verb	/vɜːrb/	/r/	road	/roʊd/
/ɑː/	arm	/ɑːrm/				/θ/	thing	/θɪŋ/	/w/	want	/wɔnt/
/ɒ/	top	/tɒp/				/ð/	these	/ðiːz/	/j/	yes	/jes/

Audio scripts

1 TRENDS

Lesson 1.1, Listening, Exercise B

1.1 **C = Carly D = Dan**

C: So? How did the job interview go, Dan?

D: It was a breeze! I got the job. But the thing is, I start in two weeks and I don't have anything to wear. The job involves meeting important clients. But they won't take me seriously in my scruffy jeans and hoodie!

C: Sounds like you need some new clothes.

D: I know. But I'm on a tight budget until I receive my first few months' salary.

C: Well, it's easy to look good without spending a fortune. Do you have a suit?

D: No, but I saw a suit yesterday for 40% off in a sale, so I'll save almost $100 if I buy that.

C: Well, you're only saving money if you buy something you really need. If you're just buying it because it's cheap, you're throwing money down the drain. It's much better in the long run to invest in timeless classics. For example, instead of buying a cheap off-the-rack suit that you'll need to replace in a few months, save up for a tailor-made suit that will make you look great for many years.

D: OK, I admit that suit was a little cheap-looking. But it was the only one in my size. They had some nice suits in the sale, but they were all too tight or too loose for me.

C: Well, you can always buy oversized clothes – as long as they're good quality, and then take them in.

D: What do you mean, take them in?

C: It's when you unpick the seams, move the pieces of fabric closer together, and sew them back together. In fact, more generally, I'd say the best way to look good without spending a lot of money is to learn to sew. But hang on a second. Didn't you have to wear a suit for the job interview?

D: Well, it was an online interview, so I just wore a jacket from an old suit and a nice shirt and tie to create a good impression. They had no idea I was wearing baggy sweatpants under my desk!

C: Haha, no, you're kidding me! It's usually a good idea to mix and match parts of different outfits, which can save you a lot of money, but I'd say mixing a suit with a sweatsuit is taking things a little far! Do you still have the pants to go with that jacket?

D: Yeah, I actually have two old suits with perfectly good jackets but pants that I can't wear! One pair is coming apart at the seams. The other is completely worn out at the knee.

C: Hmm, it sounds like you can start your sewing lessons on those pants! Then you'll have two suits in your closet for peanuts! That's actually a good example of how to go shopping in your closet.

D: Sorry. Where?

C: In your closet. Most people have a lot of clothes that they never wear. The trick is to sort them into four categories: love, mend, sell and trash.

D: Go on.

C: 'Love' is for the clothes that make you look and feel great. 'Mend' is for the clothes that you need to adjust or repair. 'Sell' is for the clothes that you can auction online. And then 'trash' is for everything else. Basically you need to get rid of them!

D: OK, I have a lot of clothes that I could sell, but I've never used an auction website before. Do you think anyone will buy my old clothes?

C: You'd be surprised. I mean, most customers on those sites stick to the professional sellers with beautiful tailor-made sales pages created by web designers. But I actually buy most of my clothes from ugly sales pages, created by inexperienced sellers.

D: What? Are you saying I should create an ugly sales page for my second-hand clothes?

C: No, not at all. The more professional your sales page, the more you can charge for your clothes. And it needs to be a seamless process for your customers from beginning to end. So as a general rule, when you're selling clothes, it's well worth taking the time to make your sales page look good. For example, you can just use one of the off-the-rack templates from the auction site. Choose a template that catches your eye – it's much better than creating your own site from scratch.

D: OK, sounds like good advice. And when I'm buying clothes online, to replace the ones I'm selling?

C: Then you should look out for newbie sellers with bad photos – they're usually good for picking up a bargain.

D: Ah, yes, that makes sense. So are auction sites the best place to pick up cheap second-hand clothes?

C: Sometimes, but the best place to buy them is usually thrift stores, even though they're pretty exhausting! You need to know where to go if you want to avoid wearing yourself out for nothing! For instance, the best thrift stores are in expensive, exclusive neighborhoods. You'd be amazed what you can pick up there. The trick is to avoid stores in a trendy area or one with a lot of students – all the best stuff will be snapped up immediately.

D: OK, good. What about regular stores?

C: They're fine as long as you're not too choosy – the big-name stores are usually no better than others, but they charge a lot more for the same stuff! But wherever you go, don't forget to haggle to get the price down.

D: What do you mean?

C: Ask the sales clerks for a discount. I always ask, 'Is this the best you can do?' Many sales clerks are authorized to offer discounts, so it's always worth haggling. You have nothing to lose but your pride!

D: OK. I'll give it a try. Thanks.

Lesson 1.2, Listening, Exercise B

1.3 **D = Dora A = Adam**

A: Hello and welcome to the latest 'Website design podcast'. Today, I've invited Dora Cho to talk about becoming a trendsetter. As I'm sure you know, Dora's video channel is the most hyper-influential source of advice on lifestyle trends on the web. Dora, are you there?

A: Sorry. I forgot to unmute Dora's microphone. Dora?

D: Hello? Can you hear me now?

A: Yes. Sorry, Dora. Should we restart?

D: You know what? Keep going. One of the most common mistakes that new vloggers and podcasters make is to expect everything to be perfect. So they edit and re-edit everything again and again. But when things go wrong, we hear the real, authentic 'you', and that's what makes your podcast engaging. You actually need to unlearn all those rules about perfection!

A: OK. But your videos are always amazing. You seem so self-confident and relaxed. How do you do that?

D: It all comes down to experience. My first videos were pretty cheesy and amateurish. I used to be fairly disaster-prone with technology: everything that could go wrong did go wrong. But after a while, it got a lot easier! I learned everything by taking risks and making mistakes. It was frustrating at the time but you need to go through that experience. I'm a lot more tech-savvy now, but I'm still learning.

A: Great. So how did you start your vlog?

D: First of all, I set myself a target of one video every week for a year. I figured that if nobody cared after a year, I'd give up. And it did take a while to get noticed, which was frustrating. But after several months, I started to see fairly big audience numbers. By the end of the year I had 7,000 subscribers.

A: Wow! And now?

D: Six million.

A: Amazing! So what am I doing wrong with my podcasts?

D: Well, there's no need to be negative. The most important thing is that you've found your niche and you've created some excellent content.

A: Really? Oh, thank you.

D: Yeah, it's true. But if you want to move to the next level, you need to be really systematic. I mean, when do your podcasts come out?

A: It depends. Whenever I have a somewhat good idea for a podcast, then I try to make it within a few days.

D: OK, but you can't expect your listeners to check your website every day on the off-chance that you've released another episode – that's not user-friendly at all. But my followers can be absolutely sure that every Wednesday at ten o'clock, there will be a new video on my channel.

A: OK. But what if you run out of ideas?

D: I won't. I plan everything at least six months in advance, and I set alerts on my phone to tell me what to do and when. I've tried to make my system idiot-proof so that I can't mess up!

A: OK …

D: You also need to be far more social media-savvy: once you've released each episode, tell the world about it. And don't just post a link – you need to engage with your audience, too, by replying to the comments on your site. People love to feel listened to.

A: Every single comment?

D: Well, there are plenty of people who post offensive or spammy comments. The trick is to ignore them and focus on the people who want to join your community. You can also ask them what they'd like you to talk about in future podcasts. Once you have an active community behind you, you'll never run out of ideas.

A: Right. OK, so I'll do all that. But it sounds like hard work!

D: It is hard work! Not long ago, a journalist mentioned my blog in an article about overnight successes. I suppose in many people's eyes, I am an overnight success. They probably think I'm super-lucky to have hit the big time. But they don't see the years of hard work behind that success.

A: Right. So I just need to keep working hard on my podcasts, right?

D: Well, your podcasts are great, as I say, but actually I think your content would work much better as smartphone-friendly videos. I mean, you talk about website design, so we really need to be able to see what you're talking about.

A: Maybe, but I'm not as charismatic as you. I hate being in front of the camera.

D: Well, I felt awkward at first, too, but you do get used to it. I really think you should rethink and become a vlogger instead.

A: OK. I'll give it a try. Dora Cho, thanks so much for joining me today. You've given me a long list of jobs to do! I feel super-exhausted just thinking about it.

2 CREATIVITY

Lesson 2.1, Listening, Exercise C

2.1 **P = Presenter C = Caroline**

P: This week's guest on *More than meets the eye* is art historian Caroline Bishop. Caroline, thanks for joining us.

C: It's my pleasure. Thank you for having me.

P: So the painting you've picked also happens to be one of the great masterpieces. Could you start by telling us its name and a little about the painter?

C: Sure. It's a painting by Velázquez, called *Las Meninas*. Velázquez is one of Spain's most important artists. He painted in a Baroque style, which means his paintings are very ornate, detailed and realistic. He mainly painted historical scenes and portraits. He painted *Las Meninas* after he'd been given a prominent position in the royal court.

P: And can you describe the painting to us?

C: Well, it depicts a scene in the artist's studio. In the center foreground we have the young Infanta Margaret Theresa, the daughter of the King and Queen – the word *Infanta* is similar in meaning to princess. The Infanta is framed on either side by her two ladies-in-waiting. Then to the right we have two other women from the royal court and a dog. Behind them are the Infanta's attendants – a chaperone and bodyguard – and further in the background, there's a royal official in a doorway.

P: OK. So, we are probably looking at the Infanta's entourage?

C: Hmm … yes we can see her entourage on the right, but to the left, we can see the artist himself, standing next to a gigantic canvas. The inclusion of the artist in the painting is one of the things that makes this such an interesting piece. It seems more like a snapshot, taken behind the scenes of the royal court, rather than the typical posed portraits of the time. It was a very original composition – groundbreaking at the time.

P: So, do you know why he chose such an unconventional composition?

C: Actually, there are several theories about this – which is one of the things I like best about the painting. There's been a lot of debate about who the subject of the painting really is. On first inspection, it seems that the Infanta is the subject – after all she's in the center of the painting. But then, if you look in the background, there appears to be a mirror that shows the King and Queen. This suggests that the artist is actually painting *their* portrait. So we, the viewer, are actually seeing the world through the eyes of the King and Queen. The Infanta and her companions are merely watching.

P: So, it's a portrait of the King and Queen, not the Infanta. Is that right?

C: Well … some people think so, yes. Even though the image of them is really small.

P: That's a very imaginative idea – and really unusual for a royal portrait I'm guessing.

C: Yes, absolutely. However … there's one other interpretation that I like. Some people believe that the scene we see is actually just the reflection in a large mirror. What we're seeing is the artist at work in his studio.

P: So this may even be a self-portrait?

C: Exactly. The point of the picture may be to show us the artist's life – this is his studio, this is what it was like when he was painting a portrait. It's actually a very complex composition. It's like a puzzle for the viewer to decide what is really happening.

P: It's fascinating – and I'm not sure which interpretation I like best. Anyway, why did you choose it as your favorite painting? Do you have a personal connection to the work?

C: Well, I first saw this painting in the Prado Gallery in Madrid over 20 years ago when I was a student. And the first time I saw it, I was astounded. It's sensational. I'd never seen anything like it. In fact, I switched to art history a couple of months later.

P: So this painting helped you to choose your career?

C: Yes, yes it did.

Lesson 2.2, Listening, Exercise A

2.5 **M = Mark L = Lauren**

L: Hi Mark, how's the dissertation going?

M: Terrible, Lauren. I'm stuck. I have no ideas today. Zero.

L: Oh, no. How awful! But did you see that article Simon shared about how people find inspiration? It's really interesting.

M: Yeah? He's always sharing self-help stuff, but…

L: No, but this one's different. It's real artists, writers, directors, musicians and dancers talking about how they come up with their ideas.

M: Hmm … So, what did they say then?

L: Oh … let me find it. Here we go. OK. This person's a fashion designer and he says, 'Inspiration can strike at any time. I sometimes get ideas when I'm out shopping or walking in the park. I always carry a pen and paper with me, so I can sketch it or write it down. Sometimes the smallest thing can trigger an idea. A flower, a smile, a color.'

M: OK. Isn't that somewhat pretentious? Can't he just use his phone to write notes? And anyway a blank notebook is still a blank notebook.

L: OK, here's an artist – he says the best time for him to get ideas is very early in the morning – when you're not exactly awake and not exactly asleep. He often sets his alarm for 4 am, so he can get into the right state of mind to have ideas.

M: What! Is he crazy? He must never get enough sleep.

L: Yeah, but come on, I know what he means. A few times, I've had a good idea just before waking up – usually when I have a problem that I'm trying to solve.

M: Well, I don't think it's going to work for my dissertation.

L: OK. But here's an actual writer. Apparently, she thinks you have to be really disciplined and get into a regular routine. You just sit down and write, because if you wait for ideas to come, you'll never do anything. She says choose a time and stick to it – even if you don't feel like it or even if your writing is terrible, you just need to shut the door, remove all distractions and write.

M: Why does she keep writing if it's terrible? I don't want my dissertation to be terrible!

L: How about this then? You should immerse yourself in other things. Do something completely different – like watch a movie. Then when you get back to your desk, you'll be refreshed and ready to be creative again.

M: That's the first thing that I agree with! I need to take a break. I think I need a change of scenery … right now.

L: Yeah, it doesn't hurt, does it? I also think it helps to talk to people – you know, bounce ideas around with someone and see if they can improve your idea. It can really help to get a fresh perspective on something.

M: Isn't that a little … scary? I don't think I want to share this dissertation until it's finished.

L: Well, it has to be someone you trust. Celia and I usually read each other's work, so we're used to helping each other. She also thinks that if you're working from a completely blank canvas, the possibilities can seem limitless, so she likes to impose some restrictions – such as using a particular genre or restricting herself to a particular format. I think she likes to set herself a challenge. That's pretty fun, don't you think?

M: OK, it's very interesting – and I guess it makes sense. It must be easier to decide what to do if you have fewer choices.

L: Yeah, and I really like the idea of giving yourself a challenge like that. There's one other thing you could do. An artist here says it's important to take risks. You might not fully understand what you're doing, but you just have to trust your instincts and run with it.

M: Is she serious? How can you make something when you don't know what you're doing?

L: Haven't you ever started doodling a picture without knowing what it was going to be?

M: Hmm … I guess so …

L: Well, I think that's what she means. So … anyway, good luck with the dissertation, Mark.

M: Thanks, Lauren!

3 PROGRESS

Lesson 3.1, Listening, Exercise B

3.1 **S = Saleswoman M = Man W = Woman**

S: Excuse me, sir. Do you ride a bike, by any chance?

M: Well, I have a bike yes. Why do you ask?

S: You just look like a very healthy and athletic person.

M: Really? Thank you. Well, I haven't ridden my bike for months. It's too wet right now.

S: Yeah, tell me about it! I bet you can't wait for the weather to warm up so you can get out on your bike, can you?

M: Uh, no. I guess not. It's not much fun biking in the rain!

S: Hmm, I know exactly what you mean. It sounds like you need some smart biking clothes.

M: Uh, sorry? I don't …

S: Smart biking clothes are made from smart materials, which change their form depending on their environment. Let me show you an example. This biking hat is made from an advanced material that responds to your body temperature. It's somewhat complicated technology, but I'll try to simplify it for you. Just imagine you're out on your bike early one morning. When you leave home, the fibers in your hat respond to the cold temperature by tightening up. That ensures there's no heat loss from your head and keeps you nice and warm. But as you warm up, the gaps between the fibers in your hat automatically enlarge to allow air to flow freely around your head, to cool you down. But then let's imagine it starts to rain. As the hat gets wet, the water strengthens the fibers and the gaps close to keep your head dry. Amazing, isn't it?

M: Yes. It sounds very inventive.

S: It is inventive! This technology is straight out of the laboratory. You won't find these in any stores for years!

M: Really?

S: No. We're still at the testing stage. Hey, would you be willing to test it for us? We'd absolutely love to hear how you do with it. It would be incredibly useful for us.

M: Uh, possibly. What would it involve?

S: You wear your hat for a few weeks while you're riding your bike, and then you fill in a five-minute questionnaire about your experiences. And of course you get to keep your hat at the end! Would that be OK?

M: Really? Yeah, why not?

S: Great! Thanks. Here's your hat. Congratulations! I just need you to sign this form to formalize our agreement.

M: OK, no problem.

S: Thanks. We're planning to sell the hats for $50 in the future, so I think you got yourself an excellent deal there, sir. I can see you're a very smart negotiator!

M: Am I? Yes, I suppose so. Thanks a lot.

S: No problem. Actually, maybe there is a problem. Did you say you never go biking in the rain?

M: Yes. Why?

S: Ah … well we really need people to describe their experiences of wearing the hat in different weather conditions over the next couple of weeks, including rain. I'm so sorry – this is really embarrassing. Should I take the hat back?

M: Uh, no. I don't mind biking in the rain once or twice. I'll just have to get a little wet, I suppose!

S: Really? Oh that would be amazing if you could. And you know what? Maybe I can help you out there. You see, we also have some smart biking jackets. They're made of tiny fibers that flatten when they're wet, making the coat completely waterproof, and they open up again when dry, enabling your skin to breathe. Again, they're not available for sale for a while, but maybe I can make an exception for you. Do you mind waiting a second while I call my boss?

M: No, not at all. Go ahead.

S: Great! Oh hi, Debbie. Listen, I have a gentleman here who's interested in buying the biking coat. I know we're not allowed to sell them yet, but … No way, huh? Are you sure? He's going to help us test our hat. Really? Oh, that's great. Thanks, Debbie! I owe you one. Good news! She says she's willing to make an exception, just for you.

M: Oh, great. Thanks. Uh, how much is it?

S: Well, we're planning to sell them for $500. But … hmm … maybe … I can offer you … a special price … to thank you for your help. I'll give you 10% off … would that be better?

M: Yes, I guess so.

S: Excellent. So that's $450, please. Will you be paying by cash or credit card?

M: Uh, credit card, I suppose.

S: Yes. Of course. Just put in your PIN here.

S: OK, perfect. Thanks. And here's your coat. Thanks so much for helping us out with the testing. I really appreciate it.

M: You're welcome. And thank you. You've been very nice. Goodbye.

S: Goodbye.

3.3 Lesson 3.2, Listening, Exercise B
P = Presenter B = Bob M = Mary
J = James C = Callum S = Sonia

P: Hello, and welcome to *The Progress Show*. According to a recent survey, despite amazing progress in technology and sharp increases in living standards, many of us believe our quality of life has actually decreased! So this week, I interviewed some people on the street about their lives. I asked them, would you say the world is generally getting better or worse? Let's hear a few extracts from those interviews.

So Bob, would you say the world is getting better or worse?

B: Worse, definitely. When I was a teenager, we always showed respect for older people. For example, no sooner had an older person gotten on the bus than we all stood up to offer the person a seat. I was on a bus the other day, and it was full of teenagers, but not one person offered me a seat. Only after they'd all gotten off the bus could I finally sit down.

P: So Mary, what's your view?

M: I'd say it's getting worse for people of my age. People of my parents' age had it much easier. There was plenty of work for everybody, and apartments and houses were much cheaper. But everyone of my age seems to be struggling for money. No way could I ever afford an apartment. It's not fair!

P: James, what do you think?

J: I feel like I'm going backwards sometimes. I mean, when I was younger, life was simple. None of our neighbors had much money, and neither did we. But we didn't need much, so we were content just to get on with life. But these days, if you don't post endless selfies of your perfect lifestyle on social media, you feel like a reject from society. It's very frustrating and stressful.

P: Callum, what's your take on this?

C: On balance, it's probably getting worse. You see such terrible things on TV all the time – crime, wars, diseases! I don't remember anything like that from my childhood. Mind you, I didn't watch much TV when I was a kid and I certainly didn't read any newspapers.

P: Sonia, how about you?

S: Worse, much worse. I remember when I was in my early twenties, life was wonderful. Not only did I have great friends, but we also did cool things all the time … and the sun always seemed to be shining. Nowadays, life's just work work work … and the weather's always terrible too!

3.4 Lesson 3.2, Listening, Exercise D
Pre = Presenter Pro = Professor

Pre: Let's turn now to my guest, Professor Nila Martinelli, an expert in psychology. Professor, is the world really getting worse?

Pro: No, not at all. However you choose to measure people's well-being, life for the average person is getting better. But the key word there is 'average'. By no means am I suggesting that life is wonderful for everyone everywhere. But the vast majority of the world's population really is better off, year after year.

Pre: OK, so why do so many people say the opposite?

Pro: Well, it's all due to a psychological process called declinism, which is a feeling that things are declining, or getting worse. Declinism has a number of separate causes, including something called the inequality paradox. Let me give you an example. Say you live in a community where everybody has terrible healthcare and education, and so on, but overall people just accept that life is hard. But now imagine that 20% of the people suddenly become a lot better off, with comfortable lifestyles and so on. Those 20% push the average up, so according to statistics, the population seems better off. But in fact the remaining 80% feel much worse than before, because they're now aware of what they're missing.

Pre: Ah. That makes sense.

Pro: Another reason is the so-called reminiscence bump. Scientists have conducted plenty of research on this subject which shows that we build up our strongest memories in our late teens and early twenties. Our memories of early adulthood stay with us for ever. This is why so many people are nostalgic for that time in their life.

Pre: Oh … so it's almost as if we rewrite the events in our memories in order to perfect the picture of our younger days!

Pro: Exactly! One of my favorite phenomena is something I call the them-and-us delusion. If you were a well-behaved child, you're likely to remember that most other kids of your age were similarly well-behaved. But that's probably because you didn't notice their bad behavior at the time. Or you've simply erased their negative attributes and bad conduct from your memory. But when you look at a group of people from the outside, what do you notice most? The noisiest, worst-behaved ones. That explains why so many people think that kids today are worse than their own generations.

Pre: Yeah, I suppose you're right. I don't remember much about my childhood!

Pro: No – and that's normal. Children simply fail to notice things that are obvious to adults. When I was a child, never in a million years did it occur to me that my parents were worried about money or job insecurity or whatever. But that doesn't mean they never talked about those things. This is something that we might call the invisible struggle phenomenon: we don't see the problems that other people face, so we think we're the only ones with such problems. We tend to attribute other people's success to luck and we overlook all the problems they've struggled with. And of course that's a major source of inter-generational conflict: young adults always suspect that earlier generations had it much easier!

Pre: Ah. I see what you mean.

Pro: There's one last aspect of declinism, and it's called the window-on-the-world effect. It arises when people become aware of the terrible things that happen around the world. Centuries ago, people were blissfully unaware of wars and diseases in distant countries. But nowadays, we see such things on a daily basis on the news, on social media and so on. So it's not that terrible events are necessarily becoming more frequent, but rather that we're aware of those events. And for me, the fact that more and more people care about global tragedies makes it more likely that we'll do something about them. And that's my main reason for optimism that the world really is getting better, and will continue to do so.

Pre: Hmm … Professor Nila Martinelli, thanks very much for joining us.

4 INTELLIGENCE

4.1 Lesson 4.1, Listening, Exercise B
H = Host Dr = Dr. Carter A = Amanda

H: On this week's episode of *Ask an Expert*, we're talking about boosting your brain power. These days many products claim to make you smarter. But is it really possible? To answer the question, I'm joined today by two experts: Dr. Ramona Carter, a leading neuroscientist, and Amanda Saraha, a life coach and the author of *How to be smarter*. Thank you for joining me.

A: Thanks, John.

Dr: Thank you, John.

H: So first up, Amanda, the big question. Can people really make themselves smarter?

A: The short answer is yes, John. But the first step may actually be believing it's possible. Researchers have shown that when a group of students are told it's possible to become more intelligent, they can retain more of what they learn.

H: Dr. Carter, do you agree? Can we make ourselves brighter? One way that's very popular is brain training games.

Dr: I have to admit, I love them. But I'm skeptical about whether they have any long-term effects. The problem is that the effects are probably not transferable. So for example, if you do a lot of Sudoku, the math puzzle where you write the numbers in boxes, it's most likely that you will just become better at playing that game.

Audio scripts

A team from Cambridge actually tried to shed some light on the impact of brain-training games. They had thousands of participants, so this was a big study doing brain training activities for at least 10 minutes a day, three times a week for six weeks. They tested them before and after. And the results showed no improvements in their test scores. In other words, their study showed that brain training didn't actually work.

A: Actually, if you don't mind me saying, that was just one study. Another study looked at older people playing a game that involved multi-tasking – they had to drive a car and look out for specific symbols as they drove. In this study, the participants showed that not only did they get better at the game, but that they also improved their attention and working memory.

Dr: Yes, you're right. But it's worth noting that this study specifically involved a video game rather than a typical brain-training game. Playing video games may affect our cognitive abilities according to research. But these kinds of games may prove to be more beneficial than dedicated brain-training games.

H: So overall, the findings about playing games are a little inconclusive right now. So, what else can we do to boost our brain power?

A: There are actually a lot of things you can do. For example, have you ever wondered why so many high achievers boast about starting the day with a workout? I strongly believe that the exercise they are doing makes them smarter and more competitive.

Dr: Well … I'd be cautious about making a direct link between high achievement and exercise, but there is a pretty clear consensus that exercise is good for the brain. Some scientists believe that exercise can help to promote the growth and formation of neurons in the hippocampus – so, as I mentioned before, if we retain the new cells that our body produces, it could affect our ability to think and remember.

H: Hmm … Is food another factor? Recently, we've seen a lot of media stories about super foods, food that you should eat to boost your brain power – fatty fish, blueberries, even chocolate. Is this true, Dr. Carter?

Dr: Um, the research is actually fairly inconclusive. Some studies have shown that eating a healthy diet has an impact on thinking ability, but claims that particular foods can impact your intelligence are mostly exaggerated or misleading.

H: Do you agree, Amanda?

A: As Dr. Carter says, we may still be in the dark about the science behind it, but I personally believe that the food we eat has a huge effect on every aspect of our lives. I know a lot of people who strongly believe that changing their diet has made them smarter.

H: OK. So maybe I do need to rethink my lunch choices. And is there anything else we can do to boost our intelligence. Amanda?

A: Well, we haven't talked about this yet, but it's actually really important to take some time out and unplug for a while. You need to disconnect from your phone and your computer and let your mind wander.

Dr: I completely agree with this. Getting enough sleep, taking some time to rest, sitting quietly or meditating has a big impact on reducing stress and anxiety, and it also helps you think. There are studies that back this up – they have shown that students who daydream do better on standardized tests than those who remain completely focused on a task.

H: So, resting can boost your brain power? That's good to know!

Lesson 4.2, Listening, Exercise B

4.4 C = Chair E = Ella

C: So the motion is: 'Intelligence gives people the greatest advantage in life.' Now I look to Ella to open the case against the motion.

E: Thank you very much. It's an honor to speak against the motion tonight. Right, it's easy to see why so many people believe being intelligent makes your life better. After all, we see intelligent people thriving at school. We see them getting into the college courses they want. We see them graduating with good academic certifications. And on top of that, we see the importance the world gives to certifications.

So, it may seem strange for me to stand here and argue that intelligent people aren't necessarily at an advantage in life. However, that is exactly what I'll do. In fact, there are several clear disadvantages in having a superior intellect.

Let's start with a lack of common sense. And let's talk about a chess champion. Not just any chess champion, but a chess champion that was also a child chess prodigy. She must be smart, right? Well, talk to her mother. According to her, she frequently locks her car keys inside her car. The 'nutty professor' – smart but absent-minded and eccentric – is a common stereotype of highly intelligent people. Some scientists believe that geniuses' brains are wired differently. While highly intelligent people are curious about complex puzzles and are able to troubleshoot, they can't deal with more mundane tasks. So Ms. Chess Champion could beat 15 chess players in a row … but she can't drive herself home.

Another problem faced by intelligent people is an inability to socialize. We've all known that friend at school or college. They're ready to answer in the physics class, they ask the lecturer countless questions and their voice drowns out everybody else's in the seminar. Then you take them to a party. Suddenly it seems like wishful thinking that anyone will talk to them again. Ever. Probably because they're still talking about physics. There are a few reasons why highly intelligent people are thought of as socially awkward. First, they find small talk tedious. You find them correcting other people's mistakes or trying to engage in a passionate debate at a casual social event. Second, they are incredibly self-conscious. This means they tend to overthink things and appear awkward.

And finally, there's the burden of expectation. You have a reputation to protect. If everyone thinks you're a genius, they expect you to be successful and make an impact in the world. Sometimes the pressure is just too much. Highly intelligent people can end up dropping out of education altogether and trying to hide their intellect to fit in. Or they're afraid to look stupid. So they avoid asking questions when they need to, or they try to skip the basics when they learn something new, which, of course, only creates problems down the line.

In summary, if you think that being smart means lounging in a bath tub waiting for a eureka moment, then think again. There are a lot of downsides to intelligence. Geniuses can lack common sense, find it difficult to socialize, and feel pressure to live up to expectations. I've always said myself that intelligence and happiness don't necessarily go together. This is no surprise to people who lock their keys in their car, don't have any friends to drive them and are too scared to ask. In fact, being highly intelligent makes life more not less difficult.

5 GAMES

Lesson 5.1, Listening, Exercise B

5.1 J = Joe O = Olga L = Lin

Part 1

J: OK, so we've been locked in. So where's the key?

L: Found it! It's at the bottom of this measuring cylinder.

J: Really?! That was easy!

L: Yeah, but there's a metal bar across the top with a combination lock attached to it. No way will we get that big key through this narrow gap.

O: So we need to figure out the combination to remove the bar, right?

L: Exactly. But even if we could do that, my arm's nowhere near long enough to reach the key at the bottom.

O: Can you tip it upside down?

L: Nah, it's attached to the wall. It can't be moved.

J: Try pulling it really hard.

O: Seriously?! That's cheating! Anyway, we'll get thrown out if anything gets broken! According to the instructions, we're not allowed to use force to move things!

J: I don't remember being given any instructions.

O: We were asked to sign a form at the front desk. Those were the instructions, Joe!

J: Ah, I wondered what that form was.

L: Didn't you read it?!

J: Uh, sorry. I just signed it.

L: Unbelievable! Anyway, there are microphones all over the place, so we're probably being listened to right now!

J: OK, so we need to get the key out of the cylinder without touching it. But that's impossible.

O: Not necessarily. Look. There's a cork attached to the key.

Part 2

O: I think the cylinder needs to be filled with water. Then the cork will float to the top, lifting the key with it.

L: Well, there's some water in this big vase, but nowhere near enough to fill that measuring cylinder.

J: What about this cooking oil? Do you think the cork will float on oil?

O: Absolutely. Bring it over here.

J: Hmm, I can't. The jug's attached to the shelf.

L: Typical! Could we use the vase to transfer the oil?

O: No. It needs to be something small enough to fit inside the jug and scoop out the oil. There must be a cup hidden somewhere. What's in that chest of drawers, Lin?

L: Let's take a look. An electric scale, a bath towel and, hmm, there's no handle on the bottom drawer. I can't open it. Any ideas?

J: Uh, maybe it'll open if we press that switch on the wall.

L: It's just a light switch, Joe! It won't … Oh amazing! You just turned all the lights off! Excellent!

J: Wait! I did it! Look up! There's a secret message on the ceiling! It must have been written in fluorescent paint – it's only visible in the dark. But it's just one word: sugar.

O: Really? There are some sugar cubes on the shelf, but how does that help us?

Part 3

L: This is ridiculous. We've been stuck in here for almost an hour. We should've been given more clues. Should we give up?

J: Give up?! No way! I told all my friends I'm great at puzzles. If we give up now, I'll be made fun of for weeks. There must be a clue somewhere – something we're missing.

O: I've figured it out! Something must have been hidden inside those sugar cubes! We need to dissolve them in water!

J: Yesss! There's some water in that vase.

O: Great! They're dissolving. And I was right. There's something there. What is it? Something metal? Aha! Two screws!

L: Screws? What are we supposed to do with them?

O: We can screw them into the holes in the drawer and use them to pull it open. Just a second.

J: You did it! You've found the cup! We're free!

L: Are you joking?! We still need to remove the metal bar from the cylinder, which means working out the combination to that lock.

J: Oh yeah, I forgot.

L: Joe! We have two minutes left! Think of something!

J: Stop yelling at me! I can't think when I'm being yelled at!

O: I suppose at least we can transfer the oil to the cylinder while we're thinking. Pass me the cup. Thanks. Ooh! There's something in the jug!

L: Yeah right! There's nothing there besides the oil. You need to get your eyes tested! Oh!

O: I was right! A glass ball. Maybe we're supposed to weigh it.

J: Great! But it's covered in oil, and so are you! Be careful not to drop it!

O: Aha, that's what the towel's for! We need to clean the oil off it first!

L: OK, but hurry up! We only have 60 seconds!

O: Calm down! OK, it weighs one kilogram 327 grams. Try that combination, Joe! One three two seven.

J: One, three, two, seven. Yes! It worked. Quick, bring the oil over! How much time do we have?

L: Forty-five seconds! Come on! Hurry up!

5.4 Lesson 5.2, Listening, Exercise C
P = Presenter

P: So? What did you make of puzzle A – the Take or Share game? The fairest outcome would be for both of you to choose SHARE, and to win $500 each. Sadly, it's more complicated than that. By choosing that option you're risking losing everything. It turns out that the best strategy in a one-round game is to be selfish, because you have a 50/50 chance of winning $1,000, which is better than a 50/50 chance of winning $500. The problem is, your opponent can be assumed to be having the same thoughts, so you'll both probably end up with nothing anyway!

This example comes from Game Theory, which involves using mathematical models to solve problems where your choices affect – and are affected by – other people's choices. It allows for more accurate predictions and estimates.

Coming back to puzzle A, things get really fascinating over several rounds, because now you can reward your partner's kindness, or punish his or her selfishness. For example, if you share the money in the first round, you're implying that you're willing to cooperate. It turns out that one of the best approaches over several rounds is to share in round 1 and then spend the rest of the game copying your opponent's previous move. However, it's important to acknowledge that this strategy doesn't always work.

Let's turn to puzzle B – the Talent Show Dilemma. If there's a clear favorite, you might conclude that voting for her would be a waste of your precious vote, because she's expected to win by a landslide anyway. Supposedly then the most appropriate solution is to vote for your second favorite contestant, to make the final more interesting. But if everyone follows the same strategy, no one will vote for the favorite, and she'll be eliminated! This type of thing is reported to have happened many times in real life – not just in talent shows, but also in important elections. So in such situations, I'd urge you to resist the temptation to vote tactically, and to vote for your own favorite.

What about puzzle C – the Food Truck problem? The answer seems obvious, right? You should put your truck at point B and instruct the other truck to move to point D – or vice versa. That way, you serve half the town each, and all the town's residents have one food truck fairly close. Wonderful, except that the other owner has no incentive to move her truck from point C. If you park at point B, she can simply assert that she's staying in her prime spot in the town center, and end up with three-quarters of the town's customers. The only way for you to get 50% is to park right next to her at point C! Even if a hundred new food trucks arrived, they'd each be better off by clustering together in a single point.

Finally, what about puzzle D – the road network? To reduce congestion, we need to build a new fast road between Smallton and Littlemarket, right? It's common sense, isn't it? But let's check. In the original network, there are two routes between the two big towns, so half the traffic is likely to choose each route. But in the new 'improved' network, there's now one obvious route that everyone's going to choose. So, it'll have almost twice as much traffic as either of the old routes, and the whole network will have much worse congestion than before!

Macmillan Education Limited
4 Crinan Street
London N1 9XW

Companies and representatives throughout the world

American Language Hub Level 5A Student's Book ISBN 978-1-380-04756-4
American Language Hub Level 5A Student's Book with Student's App
ISBN 978-1-380-04750-2

Written by Jeremy Day and Graham Skerritt

First published 2020

Designed by emc design ltd
Illustrated by Daniel Limón (Beehive Illustration) p50
Cover design by Restless
Cover photographs by Getty Images/Luís Henrique Boucault (bg), Plainpicture/Cavan Images
Picture research by Emily Taylor

Authentic video footage supplied by BBC Studios Distribution Limited
Café Hub videos produced by Sharp Focus

Authors' acknowledgements
Jeremy Day would like to thank the team at Macmillan Education for their support.
Graham Skerritt would like to thank the students who tried out activities and gave invaluable feedback. Thank you to the Macmillan Education Editorial team for your excellent comments and suggestions. And thank you to my family for your patience and support.

The authors and publishers would like to thank the following for permission to reproduce their photographs:

Alamy/Suat Gursozlu pXXIV(icons), Phillip Roberts pp16–17, Visions of America p14(b), Westend61 p2(tr); **BBC Studios Distribution Limited** pp34(a, b, c, d, e), 58(a, b); **Getty Images** p2(bl), Anadolu Agency p52, Andersen Ross Photography Inc p30(James), Axelle/Bauer-Griffin p20(bl), Peter Barritt p13, Bloomberg p37, Claudia Burlotti p30(Bob), Caiaimage/Tom Merton p45(b), Robert Daly p32, Nick David p18(tl), Lea Dettli/EyeEm pp58–59, Enrique Díaz/7cero pp10–11(background), Richard Drury p30(Callum), FatCamera pvi, Filadendron pXXVII, Flashpop pXXII, Freemixer p29, GrapeImages p5(b), Jorg Greuel p7, Paul Harris p33, Hero Images pp30(Sonia), 31, 38, Hill Street Studios p18(tr), Dave Hogan pXX, Hoxton/Sam Edwards p44(b), iStockphoto/ Ellerslie77 p1, Izusek pXXVI, Azman Jaka p4(b), Jupiterimages p45(cl), Jason Kempin p21(cm), Daniel Knighton p20(br), Roos Koole p4(mr), Justin Lewis p44(cr), Lilly3 p18(bl), Maica pp54–55, Martin-dm p9, Maskot p8, MECKY p49, Laurence Monneret p43, Jessica Nelson pXX(b), PeopleImages p42(Paul), Javier Pierini pXXI, Piola666 p15(c), Photo_Concepts p53, PhotoQuest p21(bm), Pixelfit p5(ml), Dave Porter pp34–35, Norman Posselt pp22–23(background), Tim Robberts pp42(Caroline), 56, Saenman photography p14(a), Elizabeth Salleebauer pXXIII, Skynesher p18(br), SolStock p10(t), SuperStock p15(e), Adina Tovy pp46–47(background), Tuan Tran p30(Mary), Westend61 pp3, 42(Gianni), 51, Josef P. Willems/LOOK-foto p25; **iStockphoto** p39(r); **PhotoDisc** pp40–41(background); **Rex Features/Shutterstock/**Mikael Buck p22(tl), Hufton Crow/View p16(cm), George Frey/EPA p15(d), Neil Hall/EPA-EFE p22(tr), Solent News pp26, 27(c,b); **Shutterstock/**Domino p57(illustrations), Gorodenkoff p40(bl)

Commissioned photographs in the Café Hubs by Sharp Focus pp11, 23, 35, 47, 59

Printed and bound in Brazil

2025

15

The author and publishers are grateful for permission to reprint the following copyright material: Graph from 'Vinyl LP Sales and Market Share' by British Phonographic Industry, 2017. © BPI (British Recorded Music Industry) Limited 2019. All rights reserved. Reprinted with permission of British Phonographic Industry, p6; Extract from 'Tim Smit: how we made the Eden Project' by Anna Tims. Originally published in The Guardian, 29 September 2014. © 2019 Guardian News & Media Limited or its affiliated companies. All rights reserved. Reprinted with permission of Guardian News & Media Limited, p16; Extract from 'Life In An Underwater Skyscraper' by Rex Features. © Rex Features Ltd. 2018. Reprinted with permission of Rex Features Ltd. UK, p27; Extract from 'Architect Unveils Plans For Spectacular Eco-Friendly Resort' by Rex Features. © Rex Features Ltd. 2018. Reprinted with permission of Rex Features Ltd. UK, p27; Extract from 'The 'Lily Pad City' - 03 Jul 2008' by Rex Features. © Rex Features Ltd. 2018. Reprinted with permission of Rex Features Ltd. UK, p27.